THE INNER MAP

**Navigating Your Emotions
to Create the World You Want**

Julia B. Colwell, Ph.D.

Copyright © 2020 Julia B. Colwell

All rights reserved. No part of this publication may be reproduced, distributed, or transmitted in any form or by any means, including photocopying, recording, or other electronic or mechanical methods, without the prior written permission of the publisher, except in the case of brief quotations embodied in critical reviews and certain other noncommercial uses permitted by copyright law. For permission requests, write to the publisher, addressed "Attention: Permissions Coordinator," at the address below.

ISBN: 978-0-578-69270-8

Library of Congress Control Number: 0578692708

Any references to historical events, real people, or real places are used fictitiously. Names, characters, and places are products of the author's imagination.

Front cover image by Mary Tebbs.
Book design by Tanya Leone.

Printed by IngramSpark, in the United States of America.

First printing edition 2020.

Integrity Arts Press
1637 28th Street
Boulder, Colorado 80301

www.JuliaColwell.com

ALSO BY JULIA B. COLWELL

The Relationship Ride: A Usable, Unusual, Transformative Guide

The Relationship Skills Workbook: A Do-It-Yourself Guide to a Thriving Relationship

To my students—

You challenge me to find the next best way.

We change the world not by what we say or do,
but as a consequence of what we have become.

~ Dr. David R. Hawkins

Table of Contents

The Inner Map xi

Foreword xiii

Preface... xv

Introduction:
The Inner Map 1

Chapter 1:
Nuts and Bolts of the Inner Map 9

Chapter 2:
Functions of Levels of Consciousness: Reactive Brain 27

Chapter 3:
Functions of Levels of Consciousness: Creative Brain 45

Chapter 4:
Navigating the Inner Map 57

Chapter 5:
Final Orienting Points 75

Appendix I:
Functions of Levels of Consciousness 85

Appendix II:
Four Cornerstones of Evolutionary Power 89

The Inner Map | xi

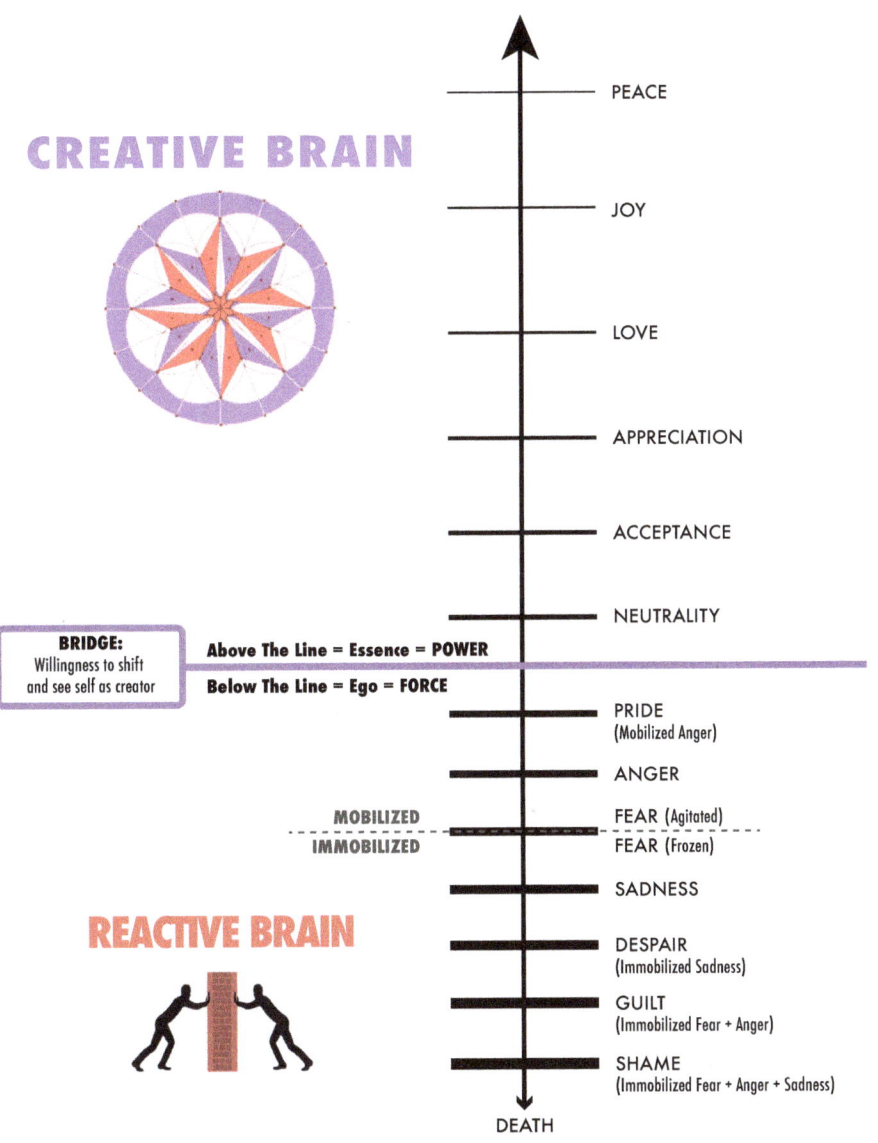

Foreword

Everything in life is made of energy. Also known as Qi, Chi, or Prana, this energy is always present; it is the soup of the world we live in. Energy can be contracted, expanded, or somewhere in between.

In our physical experience, we are manipulating these energies all of the time. We take a tray of water, cool it, and, lo and behold, we have a block. We melt the block, heat it up, and we have transformed the mass to a gas. The energy engaged with the substance changes the state. In general, we find that the less dense the state is, the more flow exists for movement.

In my almost three decades of work as an acupuncturist, combined with my decades-long meditation and contemplative practices, I have learned that these energies are not just at play in the arenas of mass. They also exist in more subtle fields. My patients have taught me that mind, body, and spirit are in a unique dance together, inseparable in motion, separable only for the use of language. In my practice, I am always and only utilizing these various densities. Assisting patients to adjust and shift into more expanded energy states supports the body in readjusting to its own natural move toward homeostasis, or balance.

In The Inner Map, Julie Colwell has taken this truth into the world of emotion. She teaches us how to locate, name, accept, and shift our emotional states. As a long-time meditator, I know that emotions are like clouds in the sky. Sometimes they appear like roaring dark beasts in ferocious storms, but they always pass. Still, like many of us, I tend to latch on to them. I hang on to the anger, the fear, the sadness, like well-worn patches on an old bomber jacket. I haven't known how to satisfactorily and efficiently work with them in ways that don't require decades of self-reflective therapy.

Julie's book has changed me. She walks us through our feelings in the most nonjudgmental and authentic of ways. She invites us into the mysterious world of our bodies—in what can often be a jungle of varied emotions—to identify our emotional states. Even more, she shows us how to become aware of our unconscious states and then how to shift them at will.

The Inner Map is not a book written from on high or some pedantic tome to set up on a shelf. It is a usable and reusable user's manual. We, as readers, are encouraged to engage, try on, and play with the concepts. Rather than just accept her model, we can test it out to decide the value and truth for ourselves. Her work is a radical approach and one that I believe has the potency to shift the way we identify with ourselves and the world at large. The Inner Map is a manifesto that leaves the reader knowing that they have the power to make a choice in the face of whatever is happening, internally or externally.

My fervent desire is to see this book and its tenets incorporated into all levels of our social, psychological, and cultural structures, enabling people to free themselves and others from the struggles and suffering of contracted, condensed energy. At the least, understanding Julie's work will allow them to recognize where they are on the Map and be able to make a conscious choice on their journey. Harmony, peaceful hearts, and compassion, both for ourselves and for others, is ultimately going to be the road home. Julie has crafted a guide to make it easier for us on our personal journeys.

Kristie Steinbock, M.S., L.Ac.
Fort Collins, Colorado

Preface

I'm writing this while still under Colorado's "Safer at Home" order due to COVID-19. Meanwhile, for the past two weeks, ever-increasing throngs of people have been marching in the streets, peacefully, powerfully, and sometimes even joyously protesting police brutality since George Floyd's death under the knee of a police officer. Folks from every sector of the United States—and, indeed, from across the globe—are clear in their conviction: Black Lives Matter.

Can you sense the seismic shift in our collective consciousness? We are coming together in a new way, stepping in and up in response to archaic hierarchical systems. The Internet has connected our global brain; a virus has demonstrated unequivocally that we also have a unified body. What impacts someone in Wuhan, China, or Minneapolis, Minnesota, directly affects me, which means this: I am directly impacting them as well. We've known about the "butterfly effect" for years, and now it is obvious every day. Humans are inextricably linked, and our evolution entirely depends upon one another.

When I was sixteen, my English teacher taught us about Existentialism (I've wondered ever since about the timing of teaching adolescents such a potentially grim reality). I was nearly undone by the possibility that there really is no point to living. While I now understand that I concluded this through a filter shaped by my adolescent difficulties and ennui (I'd put that whole experience at the level of Despair on the Inner Map), the quest to create meaning out of my life has been a daily, even moment-to-moment, preoccupation ever since. Now I understand the vast power of moving my emotions and generating my own story, how the two dance together in an ongoing flow, back and forth and up and down. I also watch how my state directly impacts those around me and then ripples beyond even those connections. Who I am is contagious. Whether we're living Above or Below The Line actually matters so much, I can see a direct line from that to whether our species, even our planet, survives.

The Inner Map is a culmination of decades of my work. I originally thought of it as a manual, a quick and concrete how-to for my students and clients to use as I taught them these concepts. It, however, apparently had its own gestational timing. Now is the perfect time for it to be born and for you to hold it in your hands—because you, too, are crucial to the health of humanity, and so to all of life.

I'd like to express my gratitude to those who supported me in writing *The Inner Map*. Truly, I could thank every person I've met, every interaction with the world I've ever had, because each experience has led me to feeling my way across the span of what I now know as human consciousness. However, that lack of specificity is unsatisfying to my body and my being on this plane. So, here are particular people I'd like to acknowledge:

Dr. David R. Hawkins, for his tremendous vision, his creativity, and the lifetime of work that went into generating his Map of Consciousness®.

Gay and Kathlyn Hendricks, for their powerful body of work that has changed the trajectory of my life and that of thousands of others'. You are towering trees who have graced us with the nourishment and shade of your ideas, wisdom, and love for decades; you are provocative trailblazers who were using body-centered practices way before the rest of the world caught on to their transformational impact.

Members of the Boulder Center for Conscious Community, especially the Intensive Learning Community and the Life Alignment Program, for their willingness to experiment with new ideas and their commitment to embodying "life Above The Line."

Marj Hahne, for her impeccability of integrity, high standards, huge heart, vast patience, and very fine-toothed comb.

My beloved, Kathryn Kucsan, for showing me it is possible to be loved no matter where I am on the Inner Map.

Julie Colwell, Ph.D.
Boulder, Colorado
June 2020

Introduction

The Inner Map

What Is the Inner Map?

Have you ever felt lost?

Like you don't know where you are, let alone where you're going?

I feel that sort of disorientation regularly. I usually center myself through meditation and intention before breakfast; but even after grounding myself these ways, something typically happens as I interact with the world that jettisons me into a totally different inner experience than I began the day with. I have felt quite flummoxed by these quick shifts. How can I feel so loving all morning and, in a nanosecond, feel angry? How in the world do I go from wide appreciation to contracted fear so fast? And when I can't shake a feeling of despair in the afternoon, how, by dinner, am I singing with joy?

Of course, such mutability is part of being human. But apart from using words and phrases like "moody" or "anxious" or "naturally optimistic," I had little language to make sense of my inner world. Like the first chemists trying to sort out elements without the periodic table, I could see differences between my states, but I had no way to make sense of how they all fit together.

I stumbled upon David Hawkins' *Power vs. Force: The Hidden Determinants of Human Behavior: An Anatomy of Consciousness*.[1] Hawkins' creation of a taxonomy of states of consciousness powerfully spoke to me. While psychologists have studied, argued endlessly about, and made huge strides in classifying emotions, Hawkins took the step of placing emotional experience into the wider realm of overall human consciousness. Further,

---

1 David R. Hawkins, M.D., Ph.D., *Power vs. Force: The Hidden Determinants of Human Behavior: An Anatomy of Consciousness* (Carlsbad, CA: Hay House, Inc., 2002).

he demonstrated how one person's inner state impacts those around them, drawing in predictable, even classifiable, reactions.

Weaving how we generate different states with how we attract certain responses from other people answers a pivotal question:

How do we create our own reality?

As if answering that question isn't important enough, Hawkins' framework takes us even further to answer another:

If we don't like the reality we're creating, what do we do to change it?

After immersing myself in the study of Hawkins' Map of Consciousness® over the past 25 years and doing countless experiments with clients, groups, and myself, I have modified it to make it more usable and to reflect current neuropsychological research. I have woven it into my foundation of feminism, psychodynamics, systems thinking, trauma theory, and neuropsychology to deepen and bring Hawkins' postulations to life. The resulting Inner Map, found on page xi, has been my go-to tool for guiding the process of transformation for my clients and myself.

Having worked with thousands of people for upwards of 50,000 hours, I feel confident sharing the Inner Map to help you:

- Identify your current state.
- Determine what you would like to be feeling.
- Take steps to shift your inner experience until you've moved to where you want to be.
- De-pathologize your experience so that you self-identify from your strengths, not from what is "wrong."
- See how your life circumstances are being generated from your inner state, so that you can focus on what will most help you change your life—that is, your state!
- Consciously choose when you want to live from hierarchy and when from co-creativity.

- Live a conscious life, where you can create what you really want to create.

I walk around with the Inner Map in my head so that, at any moment, I can check in with my body sensations and immediately discern my level of consciousness. I feel great comfort knowing where I am on the Map and understanding that, wherever I am, my state is temporary. I now see how masterful my body is at using sensations to communicate to me how I'm perceiving the world. And—the best part!—I now understand that I hold the master key: I can change my physiology, which will change my perceptions, which will alter my entire experience of reality. That is, I can change my state to change my life.

And so can you.

If you've ever been lost in a mall or an airport, locating the directory map, its big arrow pointing to "You Are Here," is the first step to finding your way. The Inner Map serves the same purpose. Paired with your ability to tune in to bodily sensations, the Inner Map orients you instantly to your current emotional state, to the actual vibrational frequency you're operating in and emitting. This feedback will allow you to see that *you* are the creator of that state. Over time, you'll observe how you're generating the states you're living in and, further, that the state you're in, in any moment, creates your entire experience of life.

As your navigation skills develop, the spectrum of states will fan out before you, like the prism our inner experience truly is. Instead of feeling "at the effect of" your emotions, you will appreciate how each level of consciousness functions to serve you. You will strengthen your ability to choose between emotions, using them to reflect how you experience the world and, ultimately, as you learn how to shift frequencies, how you want to shape that world.

Knowing Your Way Around the Inner Map

Before we dive in, let's take a quick tour of the Inner Map.

Find the Inner Map on page xi (or print your own copy[2]) and explore it. You'll see the vertical line, starting with Shame at the bottom, moving up to Guilt, Despair, and so on, all the way to Peace at the top. These states are lined up according to their amount of energy, from the most contracted (Shame, where there is very little energetic movement) all the way up to the most expansive (Peace, where there is a huge amount of energy available).

Now find the horizontal line (aka "The Line"). This is the demarcation between two distinct physiological experiences, what I've coined as "Reactive Brain" and "Creative Brain." These two groupings of states are so distinct that, going forward, I'll refer to them as "Below The Line" and "Above The Line."[3]

Now that you're oriented to the Inner Map, let's get into why you'd even want to use it.

How Will the Inner Map Help You?

My own life has been transformed through my use of the Inner Map. As you get to know it and apply it, your experience of life will change in innumerable ways:

- *You'll have more compassion for yourself (and the rest of us).*

    Humans have a rather rigid idea of what our emotional disposition should be. Somehow we're supposed to be calm, cool, and collected no matter what's going on around us. We tend to view being emotionally triggered as a failure and generally have little compassion when we or those close to us get reactive. Once you understand the Inner Map, you can truly honor reactivity for the lifesaver that it is: its automaticity and immediacy are ready to save us every time we encounter a reckless driver, a sudden curb, a persistent wasp, or any unpredictable event as we're moving along through life.

---

[2] You can download a PDF of the Inner Map at www.JuliaColwell.com/Books.
[3] As you'll find in Chapter 1, "Above" and "Below" are used for simplicity's sake to illustrate on a two-dimensional map. Expansion and contraction are more accurately depicted by the Hoberman sphere, described in the same chapter.

- *You'll stop identifying yourself with your states.*

    Shame. Guilt. Despair. Sadness. Fear. Anger. Pride. Neutrality. Acceptance. Appreciation. Love. Joy. Peace. These aren't inherent characteristics or static ways of being. They are dynamic emotional states. You're not a "depressed person"; you're in Despair. You don't "have anxiety"; you feel Frozen Fear, Agitated Fear, or Anger. You're not simply a "narcissist"; you're used to hanging out in Anger and Pride, dominating those around you. You're not just "passive"; you immobilize yourself into Guilt or Shame so as not to threaten those around you who have assumed a domineering role. In other words, with any emotion, you are reacting to a state that is, and is supposed to be, temporary. Without knowing this, it is easy to identify with a state and believe that what you're feeling defines you now and forevermore.

- *You'll understand your coping behaviors.*

    Using drugs, alcohol, sugar, or pornography; over-exercising; distracting with devices; staying busy—we all have our favorite ways to try to shift our emotional states in order to feel better. Unfortunately, most of these have side effects, lose their effectiveness over time, or cause negative consequences. Once you understand how states shift, you'll have healthier, more direct methods for feeling better.

- *Seeing others (and yourself) through a particular lens won't make sense anymore.*

    While we seem to love to explain others' (and our own) behavior as concrete, consistent personality styles, what we view as personality traits are actually descriptions of temporary states. We humans generally interface with life from an inner world that changes many times in a day. Though it may be tempting to try to pin down others' behavior through generalizations, even diagnoses, once you understand how physiology works, you'll see that how we act is the direct result of the level of consciousness we're currently inhabiting. And, even better, when you can identify that level as being Below

The Line, that is, in reactivity, you'll know the steps to take to circumvent struggle and conflict.

- *You'll know you are already whole.*

    Wholeness implies that we have a full range of emotions. Our humanness spans the great swath all the way from Shame to Guilt to Despair to Sadness on up through Fear, Anger, and Pride. It continues over The Line, from reactivity to creativity, to the more solid ground of Neutrality, Acceptance, Appreciation, Love, Joy, and Peace. If we understand that "anybody gets to feel anything, anytime, for any reason" (a principle that I teach), we have space to experience the broad expanse of our inner selves, and of life overall.

- *You'll see how your state is creating the reality you are inhabiting.*

    Some days I know that the state I'm in, and thus the frequency I'm emitting, means I probably should just stay home. For sure, until I've changed my state to being Above The Line, that is, no longer reactive, I don't try to plan anything, generate new ideas about my work, write, or solve a problem with loved ones or colleagues. Because I understand the power of my state to limit my thinking and elicit particular reactions from others, until I've shifted, I aim to keep my negativity to myself as much as possible. Once I'm back Above The Line, I'm ready to reengage in life's game of co-creativity, as I am confident I'll generate positive outcomes.

- *You'll know how to shift out of struggle and find the sweet spot of life: flow.*

    As you consciously navigate the terrain of the Inner Map, you'll experience the magic in its design. Being Below The Line means you're living in a field of resistance, where struggle and conflict thrive. And when you're Above The Line? You're living in flow, where serendipity and ease are the norm.

- *You'll become more creative.*

    We humans are encountering challenges that require new ways of thinking and new solutions. From racial and income equality to global pandemics to climate change and environmental imbalances, from government and corporate corruption to international problem-solving through militarism and force, our species is facing unprecedented difficulties. Maximizing our creativity by living Above The Line means that every single one of the 7.8 billion of us can be a resource for collectively reimagining and co-creating the world.

- *You'll increasingly view yourself, those around you, and the world as divine.*

As you inhabit the realms Above The Line (Neutrality, Acceptance, Appreciation, Love, Joy, Peace), you'll experience frequencies that the traditional means of prayer, meditation, and contemplation are designed to connect you with. Over time, you'll see that these states—which can seem miraculous or difficult to achieve—are simply part of our human design. Like discovering previously unknown floors on an elevator push-button-panel and riding the elevator there, you'll embrace your ability to move up to the top—and also down to the very bottom—knowing that true mastery of being human includes experiencing each floor, that is, tolerating, even celebrating, every energy that flows through your body.

A Note About Attractor Energies

One of Hawkins' particularly powerful concepts, "attractor energies," theorizes that, because each emotional state is made of certain electrical frequencies, different states draw in specific frequencies in response to the vibrations they are emitting. For example, if you are in a state of Agitated Fear, you'll actually attract responses that scare you even more. Shame draws forth reasons to feel ashamed. Anger pulls for a fight. Similarly, more expanded states attract expanded responses: Love attracts love. Appreciation generates appreciation. And so on.

Surveying this complex web of human consciousness, you can see how vitally important a knowledge of the taxonomy of states is for understanding how your life has been unfolding. Being adept at noticing where you are on the Inner Map and then shifting to a new state means you are truly in the rhythm of sending out and attracting back the experience you desire.

Using the Inner Map as Your Dashboard

Like the temperature gauge on the car dash, the Inner Map gives ongoing feedback about your inner world. When you are Above The Line, where your emotional and cognitive functioning purrs along, you'll know you can keep moving forward. Alternatively, when you're Below The Line, you'll get the data that you should pull over and attend to the increased friction of resistance before your engine overheats. And if you don't spot your descent Below The Line before your engine boils over, at least you'll know it's time to downshift so you can get your engine running smoothly again—and you can get back on the road to living the life you really want.

Your location on the Inner Map will indicate whether you are in the right space to solve problems, cooperate with others, generate true connection, and operate in ease and flow. Alternatively, it will signal that you need to slow down and manage your body's stress response.

YOU ARE HERE. Know where you are so you can head towards where you want to go.

Chapter 1

Nuts and Bolts of the Inner Map

Now that you have a general context for the Inner Map, let me take you deeply into the intricacies of what it is and how it works.

The Inner Map Is a Map of All Mammals' Functioning

Anyone who has experienced animals close-up—in the wild, on a farm, on TV, in the kitchen—can see that animals experience a range of emotions. From a physiological perspective, the Inner Map describes the functioning of all mammals, not just the human variety. Below The Line, an ape thumps its chest to broadcast aggression in the state of Pride; a lion roars to convey the Anger behind imminent, mortal danger; a rabbit flees in Agitated Fear but stops cold in Frozen Fear; a cow lows in Sadness when her calf is removed; a monkey curls up in Despair when taken away from its mother. Closer to home perhaps, we recognize the Guilt of a dog caught red-handed with its nose in the garbage, and we use Shame ("Bad dog!") to try to control further misdeeds, witnessing the effect of our contempt as the miscreant slinks away to a corner.

On the other side of The Line, anyone with an intimate relationship with a four-legged knows the calming nature of its ability to "just be." We are drawn to the purring of a cat, who has clearly shifted to Neutrality, Acceptance, even Appreciation of its circumstance. The eyes of a cuddling dog in the state of Love are impossible to miss, as is the Joy of a cavorting puppy. And Peace? If you're an animal lover, you certainly have experienced the deep serenity and oneness of snuggling with your warm companion. We don't yet have a way to know whether animals emit the same frequencies as humans while occupying these states, but our own matching inner experience seems to reflect that they do.

Every mammal's physiology is immediately and dramatically altered according to whether it perceives a threat and how intense that threat seems. As Stephen Porges has made clear with his groundbreaking "polyvagal theory,"[1] mammals, while in unrelenting threat, naturally move from "social engagement" (where they feel open and connected with others) to the fight/flight threat responses of mobilization, culminating in the most extreme reaction: freeze, or total immobilization.

The key difference between *Homo sapiens* and all the other warm-blooded vertebrates is our ability to use language to remember and to predict, that is, to think about the past and the future. We don't experience a state simply as electrical and chemical impulses briefly moving through the body the way every other mammal does. Instead, we feel the state, then create a narrative about it. The narrative itself serves a crucial survival function: We turn the story over in our mind and share it with others as we try to understand what happened and why. Then we use that story to predict whether and how those circumstances might happen again. Finally, we spread the word through our human pack about what we went through, supporting their survival as well.

There is a big downside to these narratives, however: *our stories anchor us into the states from which they originate.* Any good storyteller (and hypnotherapist) knows that telling a good story can re-evoke the physiology of the experience. A tingling spine, goosebumps, rising heat in chest, neck, and face—these are all indications that we, on the receiving end of the story, have taken on the narrator's emotional state. Though this can pull us into a good story on a screen or around a fire, inhabiting these reactive states, if uninterrupted, is what creates human suffering. When other mammals experience a reactive state, the state moves through their body (e.g., convulsing after freezing, or "playing dead," to survive a predator's attack), allowing the animal to move back into its normal, more relaxed physiology. When humans go into reactivity, we devise our story and tell and retell it, re-evoking the physiology of the original reactive state. This deepens the neurological groove of that chain reaction in our body, easily triggerable when a future incident resembles

---

[1] Stephen Porges, "Demystifying the Mechanisms of Trauma: Maladaptive Consequences of Adaptive Bio-Behavioral Reactions to Life Threat," UCLA Trauma Conference, March 7, 2009.

the original one. Our cultural mythologies are based on these narratives; our media recycles them endlessly. And our mental health is vulnerable to being blasted apart by them.

We are generally totally unconscious as to how our states create our narratives and how our narratives, in turn, keep us in our state, leading to a closed loop of our own making. It is easy to unconsciously stay fixed in a reality, unknowingly being the source of our stuckness, our suffering, our interpersonal conflict. We typically don't track our state and so remain unaware that we have any role in how we view the world and how it and others respond to us. Words, phrases, stories have frequencies; some anchor us in the misery of Shame, Guilt, and Despair. This is a huge difficulty for humans: *we are threatened animals who can speak.*

The good news? Now that we understand how language and narrative anchor us into particular states, we can use this knowledge to our advantage. Our language can likewise transport us to Appreciation, Love, Joy, and Peace as we generate an ongoing flow of thoughts that evoke these blissful states.

We Can Know Our State from Our Thoughts

How do you know what state you're in? Watch your physiology and its signals, internal and external, and *watch your thoughts.*

To walk through the world, we must continuously make sense of our reality. We ongoingly oscillate between the input of our sensations and how we code these sensations into our inner narratives. Beginning in infancy (and perhaps even in the womb), our very thorough cultural conditioning has provided myriad ideas we can recruit to interpret that stream of sensations into our personal meaning. For example, do you think the world is a friendly or an unfriendly place? You may have heard (or experienced) this cascade of contrasts: "The world is your oyster." "The world is dangerous." "People are good!" "People will hurt you." "A stranger is a friend you haven't met yet." "Don't talk to strangers." "Follow your heart!" "Use your head." How can you know what to believe?

We likely internalize the belief that resonates most strongly with our physiology in the moment. Since our physiology continuously changes according to what we're consuming (food, sounds, the media), what and whom we're interacting with (nature, illness, a boss or partner, a beloved pet), and how adequately our basic needs are being met (water, food, sleep, shelter), our interpretations of reality are constantly shifting. This explains how we can feel optimistic about the future in one moment, then plummet into despair in the next; and how, in connection, we open our heart and fully trust our beloveds, but then, in conflict, we can instantly shut down and demonize them.

Pretty tricky stuff, isn't it? Another way to describe our changeable experience of reality is what psychologists call "state-dependent learning": we tend to remember something best when we're in the same state of consciousness in which we learned it.[2] When we're sad, we remember the times we've felt sad before; when we're angry, we revisit past frustrating experiences. It can be a real challenge to step out of the vortex of a state and consider that our interpretation of the given moment may not reflect what is actually occurring.

Overall, humans are quite vulnerable to entering into a closed system of our own physiology, conditioned beliefs, and memories that validate our current view of reality. This is particularly problematic in the survival states of Reactive Brain, when we're at risk of acting impulsively and destructively from our most contracted beliefs about the world. For the most part, we believe ourselves ("I'm right! You're wrong!"), even though our fluctuating physiology means these perceptions are directly impacted by what we ate for breakfast, how much sleep we got, or a past trauma triggered by what we heard on the car radio on the way to work.

While this whole mechanism of creating a narrative from our shifting physiology is arguably a flaw in our wiring, it makes using the Inner Map straightforward: *Watch your thoughts and you'll know what level of consciousness you're currently inhabiting.* It doesn't matter what triggered

---

[2] The classic Psychology 101 example of state-dependent learning is this: If you habitually attend your 8 a.m. class stoned on marijuana, you'll remember the material best if you take the test at 8 a.m. stoned.

your current state. Whether it was the near-miss car accident, the article on climate change you just read, or that third cup of coffee you gulped down, simply tuning in to your thoughts ("Oh, no! I could've died!" or "We're doomed!" or "I'll never get this project done!") will lead you to knowing where you are on the Inner Map (in this case, Agitated Fear). Once you know where you are, you can decide where you want to be, and take actions to get there.

In Chapter 4, you'll learn a powerful process called Shift-and-Anchor (page 65), whereby you identify your current state (and the story behind it), feel the feelings that triggered and sustain the state, choose the state you'd like to be in, and then anchor yourself into that state through a new, equally compelling narrative. This will be a bridge to mastering your level of consciousness at any given moment and throughout your life.

Navigating the Inner Map

Once again, look at the Inner Map. Orient yourself to the vertical line. Start at the bottom, with Shame, and look up the line to Guilt, Despair, and on up, all the way to Peace.

As Hawkins postulates, these states are lined up according to *how much energy is flowing,* starting at the most contracted and proceeding up the line with less and less contraction and more and more energy flow and expansion. Shame has very little energy or movement, little more than death. (In fact, when mammals are in Shame, they are in a deeply frozen reaction, an anesthetized physiological response that is actually preparing them for death.[3]) Moving up the vertical line, you'll note, from your own experience, that each successive state has more energy and more space. Hawkins maintains that any movement up the line creates *exponentially* more energy than the state below it.

As you orient yourself, understand that "higher" is not "better," as every level of consciousness has a function; all states matter. Further, though the Inner Map you see on the page is two-dimensional, a much more

---

3 See pages 78–81 of Thomas Lewis, M.D., Fari Amini, M.D., Richard Lannon, M.D., *A General Theory of Love* (New York: Random House, 2000) for a detailed and poignant description of the physiological and often fatal ramifications of mammals in despair.

accurate model of this process is the Hoberman sphere, a geodesic-like structure that can expand out fully, then retract through its many-hinged legs until it is quite small. Shame is the most pulled-in; Guilt moves a little farther out, with its somewhat greater energetic flow than Shame has; Despair is slightly more expanded than Guilt. This progression of expansion continues up the Inner Map all the way to Peace, which presses the sphere out the farthest.[4]

What these models aim to illustrate is that a living body is an ever-shifting body, moving between greater and lesser degrees of contraction and expansion, density and spaciousness. We certainly seem to prefer the more expanded states, but to really comprehend how our body, and thus our emotional system, works is to understand that *every single state has its place in how we function in the world.* Returning to the two dimensions of the Inner Map, our human wholeness is about moving up and down, up and down, experiencing all that our body is designed to experience.

You can play around with this concept right now, noticing your own breath and how it depends on the continuous movement between expansion and contraction of your diaphragm, chest cavity, lungs, and abdomen. Over time (especially if you have practices like meditation or inner focusing), you'll notice the subtle shifts in being more open or more closed physically (and thus emotionally). Even now, you'll be able to sense this process during especially dramatic moments, when you're either plummeting from an open to a reactive state or rising out of contraction into feeling light-hearted and relaxed.

The Line: Reactive Brain Versus Creative Brain

Now look at the Inner Map and find The Line, the horizontal line dividing Reactive from Creative Brain. We'll come back to this important demarcation again and again, as it's the threshold between contracted and expanded states, between being in reactivity or in creativity.

Before we further explore the Inner Map, let me clarify what I mean by "Reactive Brain" and "Creative Brain."

---

[4] These models are simply illustrations of these concepts; they are not based on actual physical properties.

If we were to dissect a brain, we wouldn't find discrete parts that are "reactive" or "creative." Neuroscientist Paul MacLean's somewhat controversial theory about the "triune brain"[5] comes close; he postulates that the brain, evolving over millions of years, can be separated out according to function: the reptilian brain (basic functions like heart rate and breathing), the limbic system (emotions and memory), and the neocortex (higher-level, executive processes like planning and analyzing). The reptilian and limbic areas show higher levels of activation when a mammal is under threat; when threat is no longer perceived, the neocortex can be seen to come back online.

More generally, the nervous system has two complementary processes: the acceleration provided by the sympathetic nervous system and the braking generated by the parasympathetic nervous system. Like driving a car, these two systems activate a continuous stream of "go" and "stop" signals that allows everything happening in our body (e.g., heart rate, respiration, hormone production, digestion, cognition) to hum along in harmony. However, when we don't have the emotional and physical resources to "up regulate" when we need to get activated or "down regulate" when it's time to rest, our engines are likely to to into overdrive—or do a dead-stop.[6]

When I use the terms "Reactive Brain" and "Creative Brain," however, I am not referring to particular areas of the brain or the aforementioned aspects of the nervous system. My terminology is more global, referring to two physiological modes of mammals (threat and relaxation) and the range of emotional states within them.

Let's start with that notorious troublemaker, Reactive Brain. *Anytime* we perceive a threat[7], we go into Reactive Brain. This brilliant evolutionary design has ensured the survival of the human race over millennia. Perceiving threat is automatic, rooted in everything we've learned about the world since we were born. It isn't a conscious process; it's unconscious and immediate, so that we can react without thinking about it. You're alive

---

[5] Paul D. MacLean, *The Triune Brain in Evolution: Role in Paleocerebral Functions* (New York: Springer, 1990).
[6] Robert M. Sapolsky, *Behave: The Biology of Humans at Our Best and Worst* (New York: Penguin Books, 2017), p. 26.
[7] Note that perceiving a threat does not mean a threat is occurring.

today because of your Reactive Brain's ability to immediately compel an action. How many times have you jumped out of the way of a bus, or jerked the steering wheel to avoid an obstacle in the road, or leapt away from a snake on the trail, or run from a menacing figure in the dark? Your Reactive Brain has enabled you to survive.

How do you know you're in Reactive Brain? Your body gives you all kinds of signals, but the clearest is this: you don't feel very good. The stress hormones coursing through your body may make you feel adrenalized and focused, but you don't have the sense of relaxation and ease that are the hallmarks of Creative Brain.

As you tune in to your own experience of Reactive Brain, you'll observe the wide range of physiological signals it sends out to get your attention. First, you'll notice subtle cues: maybe a slight nausea, muscle stiffness, a quickening pulse, shallower breathing. As your reactivity intensifies, you'll be aware of more obvious signals, such as a full-out racing pulse, contraction of your muscles, narrowing of your vision, increased blood pressure, and other symptoms of the classic fight/flight/freeze responses. Recognizing that your Reactive Brain has come online is the first step to befriending it, with the ultimate goal of discerning where on the Inner Map your body has taken you.

As I said earlier, the Reactive Brain states of Shame, Guilt, Despair, Sadness, Frozen Fear, Agitated Fear, Anger, and Pride are lined up according to how much energy is moving in them. From the highly clenched collapse of Shame, to the slightly more energized Guilt, on up to the invigorating righteousness of Pride, there is a marked difference in how much movement occurs in each state. Meanwhile, each state is saddled with the costs of the basic requirement of reactivity: being in a stress response.

Now let's swing our focus to the zone of Creative Brain, Above The Line. So much changes as you move out of Reactive into Creative Brain. Whereas Reactive Brain directs the body to react urgently and automatically by contracting muscles and vision, Creative Brain tells the body to relax and take its time. Your muscles loosen, your breath deepens, your blood pressure drops, and your vision broadens and expands. Your thoughts are creative and much clearer, and your choices become conscious, not hampered by the repetitive, stale, conditioned thinking that is a sure sign of Reactive Brain.

Like the states Below The Line, those Above The Line (Neutrality, Acceptance, Appreciation, Love, Joy, and Peace) progress along a continuum of density to expansiveness, but the latter all have the clear physiological baseline of a growth, not a protection, response.[8] As soon as you shift into Creative Brain, your relaxed physiology allows for heightened creativity, illuminating and enabling new possibilities. Your relaxed Creative Brain orients you towards connection and collaboration with others, unlike your guarded Reactive Brain, which judges, from moment to moment, whether others are "friend" or "foe." (As I mentioned earlier, this rapid shift is puzzlingly familiar to anyone who has been triggered by their intimate partner. One moment, the other is the beloved; the next, the enemy. Trying to figure out which is "true" and choosing to believe Reactive Brain is the root of many a relationship's demise.)

Qualities of Reactive Brain Versus Creative Brain

How we function in Reactive Brain and how we function in Creative Brain are worlds apart. Here are some ways to discern which brain you're in:

Reactive Brain:

- You have a narrow focus[9]; your attention is on what is "wrong."
- You have a sense of immediacy and urgency.
- Your thinking is stereotypical and concrete.
- You're basically "cognitively disabled," as your body puts its resources into fighting, fleeing, or freezing from the threat.
- Your energy, while initially charged up to respond to threat, is ultimately being depleted.

---

8 Bruce H. Lipton, Ph.D., *The Biology of Belief: Unleashing the Power of Consciousness, Matter, and Miracles* (Carlsbad, CA: Hay House, Inc., 2008), p. 149.
9 Les Fehmi, Ph.D., and Jim Robbins, *The Open-Focus Brain: Harnessing the Power of Attention to Heal Mind and Body* (Boston: Trumpeter Books, 2007), p. 14.

- Your body is in a stress response, releasing a surge of hormones, predominately adrenaline, cortisol, and norepinephrine.
- Your immediate focus is on what the threat is and who is causing that threat (i.e., who is to blame).
- Your speaking rhythm changes: either it speeds up and sounds forceful or language is hard to find and hard to generate.
- Life seems difficult, full of effort and struggle, as you are existing in a field of resistance.
- You feel disconnected from others.
- You perceive the world through a lens of competition, scarcity, and unfriendliness.

Creative Brain:

- Your focus will be open while your attention tunes in to what is "right."[10]
- You experience time as slowing down and expanding.
- The quality of your thinking is optimized, allowing you to generate new possibilities and innovative ideas.
- Your energy is being continuously regenerated.
- Your body is in a relaxed, rebuilding response, as cells can shift away from protection and into regeneration.
- Your speaking pace is natural, easy, and unpressured.
- You perceive others as safe, as potential collaborators and allies.
- You're in a field of expansiveness, in ease and flow; life unfolds with serendipity.
- Your sense of connection with others is enhanced.
- You perceive the world as being full of kinship, abundance, and friendliness.

---

10 Not as in "right/wrong" but as in "all is well."

As you become accustomed to listening to your body's sensory feedback, you'll find that it immediately tells you whether you're in Reactive Brain (Below The Line) or Creative Brain (Above The Line). I want to remind you that Reactive Brain isn't "bad," nor is Creative Brain "good." *Every state you've experienced has supported you to be here today.*

As you let yourself fully experience the range of states of Reactive Brain (Shame, Guilt, Despair, Sadness, Frozen and Agitated Fear, Anger, and Pride), you'll see that *your physiology not only tells you what state you're in but ultimately determines your actual experience of reality.* For example, as your body generates the near total contraction of Shame, you'll see that your thoughts—that is, the stories you're telling yourself—will be shame-filled, directly reflecting that state. As your body moves into somewhat less contraction, to Guilt, you'll be able to detect this through your guilt-filled thoughts. Your body in Despair will generate stories about giving up, and so on, up the vertical line. Further, your state will be contagious to those around you and will predictably determine how they interact with you. This is how you create from your state, as the outcomes of your life are a direct result of the emotional states you inhabit. Your emotional state is the most powerful determinant of your experience of the world.

While many theories and techniques in the field of psychological change focus on identifying the origin of Reactive Brain states (i.e., talking about where they come from with the intention of healing through understanding), I don't see that strategy as being the most effective. For the most part, talking about a state simply re-evokes the state. Instead, I'd like you to develop this profoundly life-altering skill, the ability to

- notice your physiology,
- question the stories generated by that physiology, and
- shift your physiology to a new, more expanded state, where your thinking will automatically become more positive.

Now let's look at the ramifications of Reactive Brain versus Creative Brain.

Reactive Brain supports hierarchy; Creative Brain supports co-creativity.

Perhaps my most profound discovery in using the Inner Map has been that Reactive Brain is not just the system running the mammalian response to threat; it is also the endoskeleton of hierarchy. In the next chapter, where I describe each state Below The Line, you'll see how the mobilization of the upper reactive states (Pride, Anger, Agitated Fear) is paramount in triggering the immobilization of the lower reactive states (Frozen Fear, Sadness, Despair, Guilt, Shame)—and vice versa. The instantaneous, urgent reactions of states Below The Line work together beautifully. Mobilization reactions are the equivalent of domination, leading to the instant submission of others through immobilization. Conversely, submission tends to activate a mobilized, dominating response from others. This linked reaction is clear in an emergency situation, when one person may mobilize to lead while others immobilize as they comply. This is a key element of how humans have survived over millennia.

In other words, hierarchy serves the extremely useful function of keeping social order. We go in and out of hierarchy all day long, obediently standing in line, sitting in classes, or following directions from authority figures. Or we might step into leadership roles, directing and teaching children, or executing plans with those who are "lower" on the chain of command where we work.

Unfortunately, what is efficient in emergencies or in circumstances necessitating supervision requires emotional disconnection both from ourselves and from those we're relating with. Mobilizing into leading or immobilizing into following removes us from our own inner experience as we go on automatic pilot into, respectively, the energy surge that domination requires or the energetic repression necessary for submission. This temporary disconnection from our inner world means we are also unable to emotionally connect with anyone else. Hierarchy is fast and efficient, but at the cost of intimacy.

This lack of internal and external contact can easily lead to conflict and escalation. The domination/submission patterns of Reactive Brain collide with our human need for affiliation when the emergency has passed and emotional intimacy is sought. What was adaptive while a threat was present can be difficult to shift out of when the threat has subsided, all the more problematic since we often get triggered into Reactive Brain when no danger is actually present. Because we humans typically have little awareness of our emotional states and the myriad unconscious ways we're broadcasting these states to others, we often end up getting stuck in power struggles in our relationships. Until these dynamics become conscious (or until we naturally shift back into Creative Brain), our whole functioning—physical, emotional, cognitive, and relational—is "at the effect of" patterns that are instinctive mammalian reactions.

Meanwhile, Creative Brain awaits. Once the perception of threat has passed, we'll naturally shift back into a relaxed state, where our healthy functioning can resume. We can now perceive others as allies, thus allowing us to reconnect with them. Cognition clears and we become creative again, leading to innovative thinking, renewed energy for problem-solving, and new engagement with collaboration and co-creativity.[11]

Reactive Brain is resistance; Creative Brain is flow.

A fundamental distinction between Creative Brain and Reactive Brain is the field of energy they occupy. Hawkins stresses this in how he distinguishes "power," which is Above The Line (Creative Brain), from "force," which is Below The Line (Reactive Brain). The hierarchy that is part and parcel of Reactive Brain occurs through the control and force that dominators exert, thereby eliciting submission in others. This force must be ongoing (or at least perceived to be so) or hierarchy will be interrupted. However, no one will be willingly controlled over time. Foot-dragging, "forgetfulness," and other signs of passive-aggression are all-too-familiar responses to anyone who is supposedly "in charge."

Because of this built-in power struggle of Reactive Brain, *all states of Reactive Brain use up energy*. It takes energy to dominate (as we "push"

---

[11] Because we instantly become hierarchical when reactive, no human believes in equality when in Reactive Brain, though equality is our natural experience of others when we're in Creative Brain.

others around); it takes energy to submit (because we have to quell our impulse to act). This collective energetic push/pull is another hallmark of Reactive Brain. This is the field of resistance.

Alternatively, there is no resistance in Creative Brain. Each of us can step forward into our full expression. Because of this built-in flow, *all states of Creative Brain generate energy.* Our energy field expands into co-creativity with those we're interacting with, and then beyond, interfacing with the creative energies of the universe.

Reactive Brain is density; Creative Brain is expansiveness.

You know by now that our brain is constantly scanning for threats to our survival. When it finds something, it sends out the alarm through stress hormones, setting off a chain reaction of automatic physiological responses to handle the threat, like increases in pulse rate, blood pressure, and muscle tension, as well as many others. If we aren't able to fully express our anger, fear, or sadness as these effects are taking place, they'll leave an energetic trail in our cells, accumulating over time. This accumulation is what gets triggered down the road when we experience an event we unconsciously code as similar. We feel these triggers as dense or contracted sensations, like neck tightness, a knotted-up stomach, or a heavy heart. While such sensations may reflect what is happening currently, they may also be the artifacts of past experiences. This density can be moved out of the body through particular expression or energetic practices.[12]

Alternatively, the states of Creative Brain don't leave any energetic byproducts. Their qualities of calmness, relaxation, groundedness, open-heartedness, and effervescence are, in fact, the antidotes to the stressful nature of Reactive Brain. Energetically enfolding Agitated Fear with Love, or Despair with Acceptance, or Pride with Neutrality will clear and shift the density of any state of Reactive Brain, supporting the body to experience the flow and true power of Creative Brain.

---

[12] Relationships often serve as an excellent catalyst for the movement of old density out of the body, as we get triggered into past states by what is going on currently within intimacy.

Reactive Brain is ego and persona; Creative Brain is essence.

In spiritual circles, "ego" has a bad reputation. It's clear that humans are supposed to surpass the ego to access higher realms. But have you ever wondered what the heck an ego is? I'd thought my ego's taking over was like some unevolved, sneaky part of me creeping in under cover of darkness. I wouldn't know why it would insinuate itself into my life; I just knew I was supposed to ward it off.

Now that I understand Reactive Brain and Creative Brain, I see that Reactive Brain *is* the ego. Every level of consciousness Below The Line (Pride, Anger, Agitated Fear, Frozen Fear, Sadness, Despair, Guilt, Shame) is a signal that we're disconnected from our true, authentic self, operating from a conditionedsurvival response. In different parlance, we have "personas"[13] at each of these states, roles we learned along the way to handle survival threats. Valuing, again, Reactive Brain for keeping us alive, let's take a moment to celebrate all of these states and appreciate the ego, that is, Reactive Brain in all of its forms.

I'm guessing you know where I'm going with Creative Brain. Indeed, Creative Brain reflects who we were when we came into this world. It's our authentic, true, essential self, all of those attributes that connect with our deepest, purest aspects, our gifts, our naturally born, infinite well of creativity. It is our divinity.

Reactive Brain is victim consciousness; Creative Brain knows we are Source.

When our Reactive Brain scans for a threat and finds one, that threat appears to be coming from outside of us, making us the victim of circumstances. The overdue bill, the interaction with our surly boss, our partner's anger, getting sick—the list is endless of what can go wrong. And does.

Here we discover why the step over The Line is such a big shift in

---

13 For more on working with personas, see Gay Hendricks, Ph.D., and Kathlyn Hendricks, Ph.D., *At the Speed of Life: The Power of Body Intelligence to Create Transformational Magic* (Ojai, CA: Hendricks Institute Publishing, 2019), as well as my book *The Relationship Ride: A Usable, Unusual Transformative Guide* (Boulder, CO: Integrity Arts Press, 2012).

consciousness. The more you live Above The Line, the more you'll know yourself as the source of your experience, no longer "at the effect of" life. As psychologist Lisa Feldman Barrett makes clear in her groundbreaking book, *How Emotions Are Made: The Secret Life of the Brain*[14], there really is no "there" out there. You are the origin point of your sensations, and then of your interpretation of those sensations into emotions, and then of your narrative about it all. And, as you're learning in this book, this process culminates in both attracting a particular set of responses and creating your own version of reality.

Reactive Brain is "mind"; Creative Brain is heart and soul.

Locking children in cages with concrete floors. A $700 billion military budget in the face of nuclear proliferation.[15] Sexual assault. Police brutality. Mass shootings. Each of these socially abhorrent outcomes makes sense through the lens of Reactive Brain. Remember that, whatever our level of consciousness is, we believe ourselves and, from that state, attract a reality that matches it. All perspectives and behaviors make sense, then, if we know the state someone is in when they're making decisions.

As I learned many years ago from a wise teacher, Gail Kali, "the mind does not wish the best for you." She meant the mind generated from the projections of Reactive Brain, which will always interpret reality from a place of threat. While helpful for survival, this instinct catalyzes the chain reaction of sensation/projection/emotion that culminates in our experience of a hostile world. It is Reactive Brain that generates a narrative of an unfriendly universe, leading to our own suffering as well as that of those we draw into that narrative. All attacks of other (and self) originate from this threatened brain, which justifies its propensity for cruelty, from criticism to physical abuse to atrocity and genocide.

But then there's Creative Brain, waiting to take us (and thus the people around us) into an entirely different experience of reality. As we move

---

14 Lisa Feldman Barrett, *How Emotions Are Made: The Secret Life of the Brain* (New York: Houghton Mifflin Harcourt, 2017).
15 Office of the Undersecretary of Defense, *National Defense Budget Estimates for FY 2020*, May 2019, https://comptroller.defense.gov/Portals/45/Documents/defbudget/fy2020/FY20_Green_Book.pdf.

through the states Above The Line, we increasingly relax and expand. These higher states allow us to access our true self, those essence qualities that come through when we're not acting from the personas of Reactive Brain. We can connect with our heart, that is, our truths arising from our deepest beingness. And we can express our soul, those essential aspects we came into this world with, as we generate a life aligned with our innate gifts. If we inhabit hell when we're in Reactive Brain, heaven is just a step over The Line, back in Creative Brain.

Craft Your Ability to Shift Your State

As you play with noticing your inner state, you'll also discover what it takes to shift from one state to another. Reactive Brain necessarily relies on stress chemicals (e.g., adrenaline, cortisol, norepinephrine) to instantly arm the body to deal with threat. Shifting into Creative Brain is actually quite simple: it requires only the metabolization of these chemicals. There are countless ways to do this, called "shift moves" by Kathlyn Hendricks[16]: breathing, making funny faces, dancing, singing, running, petting a dog, loving what is, tuning in to sensations and describing them, noticing the environment, sleeping—anything that will return the body to its natural well-being. Please note that TALKING ABOUT THE ISSUE is *not* a shift move. Talking tends to anchor us into our current reactive emotional state and escalate the internal or external situation.

Chapter 4 presents several processes that will powerfully build your state-shifting muscle. Here you'll learn how to train your mind to focus on life-enhancing thoughts and stories, as well as how to anchor yourself into higher and higher levels of consciousness.

As you experience the increasingly expanded states of Creative Brain, you'll find your rhythm with what it takes to open to that expansion, as well as with what you might do to interrupt it (if you're feeling *too* good). With practice, you can change what is happening in your body and, thus, how you are perceiving and then impacting your own experience of the world. It's not "better" to live Above The Line, but it sure is easier!

---

16 Kathlyn Hendricks, Ph.D., Foundation Workshop, Santa Barbara, CA, January 2004.

Chapter 2

Functions of Levels of Consciousness: Reactive Brain

Inside the dichotomy of Reactive Brain and Creative Brain, every level of consciousness can be sorted into its discrete function. While emotional states may appear to simply be reflecting the various hues of human experience, when studied carefully, they each reveal their particular reason for being part of our repertoire. We can thank the economy of nature for this, as it is designed such that everything has a purpose. Now that you better understand the context of Reactive Brain and Creative Brain, let's explore the actual function of each state.[1]

Refer to your copy of the Inner Map as I describe every level of consciousness and what it does for us. Because our general aim as conscious beings is to move up the vertical line, I usually present the states in ascending order (from Shame on up); however, to illustrate how the Reactive Brain states work together to maintain social order through hierarchy, we'll begin right Below The Line, with Pride, the most mobilized (and expanded) state of Reactive Brain, then move all the way down to Shame, the most immobilized (and contracted) state. As we travel through these states, you'll see how every one of them is actually just some combination of the three primary survival emotions: anger, fear, and sadness.

To illustrate the power of our stories to anchor us into a level of consciousness, I've added, at the end of each level's description, the thoughts of two ongoing narratives. Person #1 is the voice of someone dealing with self-esteem issues; Person #2 is the voice of someone navigating their beliefs about the impact of climate change on the future of our planet. As you move down through the levels of consciousness of Reactive Brain, you'll notice the progressive increase in immobilization, victimization, and powerlessness that come from living in those states.

---

[1] The functions of the Reactive Brain and Creative Brain states are summarized in the charts in Appendix I on pages 87–88.

PRIDE

A proud man is always looking down on things and people: and, of course, as long as you are looking down, you cannot see something that is above you.[2]
~ C.S. Lewis

The function of Pride is to solidify the status of the alpha.

Pride is the state of Reactive Brain that holds the most expanded energy. Pride, in this context, is not a reflection of true self-confidence and valuing of self. That type of pride is actually the trust in oneself that is the natural result of being able to maintain oneself Above The Line and to increasingly live from essence.

Instead, Pride that exists Below The Line reflects self-righteousness, a perception that we are superior to others. Our thoughts are filled with our preeminence, with what is right about us and what is wrong with other people (and all other beings in general). The concept of human dominion is anchored in Pride, as is white supremacy, male supremacy, racism, classism, ageism, sexism, and the like.

Pride is fueled by the survival emotion of mobilized anger, but is a more refined, more expanded state than the pure aggression of Anger, the next level down. Pride is communicated mainly through contempt, broadcast in facial expressions (eye-rolling, specific grimacing), vocalizations (tongue-tsking, back-of-the-throat clicking), and put-downs.[3] You know you're in Pride when your posture is stiffly erect, your chest is puffed out, and you feel energy moving through your whole body.[4] Your lips may curl into a snarl as your arms cross and you lean your weight on one leg. Your speaking tone tends to be loud and punctuated for emphasis. Your thoughts are focused on how you (or your tribe) are right, and the other (or their tribe) is wrong. You spend many emotional and relational resources developing theories to support your stance.

---

[2] C.S. Lewis, *Mere Christianity* (New York: HarperOne, 2015), p. 125.
[3] The 45th president of the United States is a master at using contempt to immediately put others "in their place."
[4] As I present the signals of these states, you'll notice that most, if not all, are innate. However, as Lisa Barrett Feldman discusses in *How Emotions Are Made: The Secret Life of the Brain* (New York: Houghton Mifflin Harcourt, 2017), some may be culturally conditioned.

These expressions of contempt allow the alpha, the leader of the pack, to keep their status without resorting to actual aggression. Recall the lion's roar, the gorilla's chest-beating, the wolf's bared teeth. There is no question to those lower in the hierarchy what will occur if they do not submit. They instinctively understand that to not comply is to risk inciting the wrath of the alpha or their lieutenants (that is, those supporting the alpha's status in the hierarchy).

There is a strong motivation for humans to stay in Pride: to give up Pride is to risk plummeting all the way down into Shame. "Pride goeth before a fall," right? Conflicts in relationships often escalate because of this connection between these two states. While there can be much egoic satisfaction in feeling the Pride of being "right," there is even more relational pressure to not feel the Shame of being "wrong," as admitting you're wrong may beget the other's contempt and, in turn, your humiliation. One way out of this incendiary standoff is the runaway ramp of this question: *Would you rather be right or happy?* A long-term commitment to choosing happiness over being right can absolutely transform the quality of a relationship.

Now, let's see what our two sample people say to themselves or others when they're in Pride:

Person #1 (self-esteem issues):
What is wrong with everybody?! Why are they so stupid?! Now *I* should see someone to talk to? That's ridiculous. They need to pull it together and stop being so soft. What a bunch of suckers.

Person #2 (climate change):
I recycle; I don't fly anymore; I drive a Prius. What's the matter with everyone else?!

ANGER

The Queen turned crimson with fury, and, after glaring at her for a moment like a wild beast, screamed, "Off with her head!"[5]
~ Lewis Carroll

The function of Anger is to directly establish and maintain the status of the alpha through pure, direct, mobilized aggression.

Anger is the energy of domination. Rams locking horns, countries threatening or using military force, a boss dressing down an employee in a meeting, parents yelling at their kids—there is no mistaking the energy of direct Anger.

Anger's energy moves up and out. While some view Anger as a secondary emotion, I believe Anger has two very important survival functions: To stop intrusion ("NO!") and to move through obstacles ("UMPH!"). In other words, *Anger stops what we don't want, and pushes to get what we do want.* You know you're in Anger when your pulse is racing, your blood pressure is rising, and you feel an impulse to push. Your jaw may be clenched; and your mouth, contracted (consider the jaws of a growling dog). Your eyes may be flaring as you glare directly at the perceived threat. Energy is coursing through your limbs, and your fists may be clenched or raised. Your speech is loud and overpowering, truly designed to frighten others. Your thoughts are only about how to dominate, how to overpower and prove the other wrong, that is, make them submit.

Of course, when we're in Anger, someone else usually is, too. This is the essence of a power struggle. We push, the other pushes back, we push again, the other pushes back, on and on, until finally one "wins," overpowering the other into submission. Hierarchy is kept intact. This type of power struggle is at the heart of an intimate relationship that lapses into violence as the couple's bodies are instinctively pulled into expressing more and more aggression until one partner finally submits. It also explains the escalation to the madness of armed conflict.

Let's check in with what our sample people are thinking when they're in Anger:

---

[5] Lewis Carroll, *Alice's Adventures in Wonderland & Through the Looking-Glass* (New York: Bantam Dell, 1984), p. 65.

Person #1 (self-esteem):
I hate everyone! They are making my life miserable! I just want to punch somebody!

Person #2 (climate change):
I am *so* sick of these corporations ruining the planet! I want to find one of those CEOs and murder them!

A Note About Pride and Anger

Pride and Anger are levels of consciousness that we traditionally think of when we imagine what "power" looks like. However, while these states may appear to be powerful, they exist in a field of resistance, making any ability to actually accomplish something quite shackled. When I push, you will instinctively push back, making movement forward much more arduous. As I said earlier, hierarchy works very well in emergencies and other times when the prevailing need is social order. For example, if there's a sudden loud sound, we instinctively orient to it and look for any signals about what to do. If an alpha clearly and aggressively instructs us into action, our bodies naturally submit and follow. We slow down when we see an accident on the side of the road and willingly follow the police officer's direction. We abide the teacher's instruction to open our books. Once the circumstance at hand is over—the source of the loud sound is determined and handled, we drive past the accident, we exit the classroom—the instinct for hierarchy recedes. The initial submission subsides, and our real self steps back in. We resume the role of being in charge of our own life.

Because of our traditional reliance on hierarchy as the primary mode of governance, though, Pride and Anger seemingly have the most value and greatest human advantage as states of being. However, the fact that they are Reactive Brain states demonstrates their cost. Like every other reactive state, Pride and Anger require the mobilization of stress chemicals, making these states physically unhealthy and cognitively expensive for their host. And because of the human disconnection intrinsic to hierarchy, those who exist primarily in Pride and Anger have difficulty creating truly authentic relationships.

Further, while domination and submission may seem efficient, over time they lose steam. We get tired of being in charge and lose respect for those "under" us, seeing them as inferior and childlike. Alternatively, we get sick of being dominated, controlled, and disrespected and will eventually rebel directly or secretly. Even if we submit for a while, ultimately *our true self must be expressed*. If the self isn't expressed directly, it will find a way to make itself known indirectly, through passivity, inertia, resistance, or manipulation. Ask any parent if they feel powerful, and you'll understand the energetic cost of trying to keep others "in their place."

There is another relational cost of hierarchy. In an intimate relationship, the person who is "power up," that is, in the dominant position, tends to stop being attracted to (and in love with) the person who is "power down," the subordinate. Power Down typically admires the strength of Power Up, but at the cost of their own sense of self. Over time, this combination is quite toxic to the relationship, as Power Up tends to exist in a zone of irritability and criticism, while Power Down typically drifts into depression and a lack of identity. Under these circumstances, Power Down is quite vulnerable to being drawn to others outside of the relationship, where they can rediscover what it feels like to be valued and respected by another.[6]

AGITATED FEAR

> *Take it from me: If you hear the past speaking to you, feel it tugging at your back and running its fingers up your spine, the best thing to do—the only thing—is run.*[7]
> ~Lauren Oliver

The function of Agitated Fear is to get to safety.

Agitated Fear is third in the line of mobilized responses. After Pride moves to Anger, it further contracts to Agitated Fear, where the instinct to get the heck away from danger exists. Agitated Fear uses the more focused, aggressive energy of Anger to take what is actually the smartest action for a wild animal: flee.[8] Animals in the wild would much prefer to get away

---

6 You can read much more about these dynamics in my book *The Relationship Ride: A Usable, Unusual, Transformative Guide* (Boulder, CO: Integrity Arts Press, 2012).
7 Lauren Oliver, *Delirium* (New York: HarperCollins, 2011), p. 176.
8 Thomas Lewis, M.D., Fari Amini, M.D., Richard Lannon, M.D., *A General Theory of Love* (New York: Random House, 2000).

than engage in battle with each other, as the threat of being wounded could be fatal. But if the preyed-upon animal were blocked from fleeing, it, now trapped, would move back to the aggression of Anger, snarling and lunging to try to dominate its way out of danger. Thus, the state of Agitated Fear is tremendously functional because, while it appears to be a power-down position, it allows mammals to escape and thus survive.

The signs of Agitated Fear parallel those of Anger, though the energy is channeled into fleeing (and otherwise protecting) instead of fighting. You know you're in Agitated Fear when, in addition to a sped-up heart rate and high blood pressure, the blood flows to your limbs, and your clenched fists want to pump into running. Your speech is still loud, but it's oriented away from others. Your thoughts are fast and single-focused: you can't think about anything else but getting away.

Because our mammalian survival instinct is coded into our DNA and thus inextricably woven into our human body, I urge you to find some way to follow your natural impulse to run away when you're in Agitated Fear. Get up and power-walk to the bathroom. Go outside and skip around (or do what I occasionally do and full-out run down the street). As I remind people over and over, *when in Reactive Brain, the only thing to do is get back Above The Line, into Creative Brain*. Simply expressing the state—so far, by pushing against something when in Pride or Anger, and by running when in Agitated Fear—will allow the body, in its innate wisdom, to discharge the reactive energy and naturally move up the vertical line.

Here's what our sample people are thinking when they're in Agitated Fear:

Person #1 (self-esteem):
What should I do?! I don't know what to do! My life is falling apart! I'm going to fail! Oh, no! What should I do?!

Person #2 (climate change):
The world is coming to an end! There's nowhere to run! It's too late! We're doomed!

A Note About the Transition from Mobilization to Immobilization

A crucial shift occurs between Agitated Fear and the state below it, Frozen Fear. Up to now, reactivity has been mobilized, from Pride to Anger to Agitated Fear. There is tremendous energy in each of these states, expressed externally to either dominate or escape. However, in Frozen Fear, there is now *immobilization*. The energy that activated Pride, Anger, and Agitated Fear now changes its direction from outward to inward. This immobilization, or submission, intensifies with the downward progression Below The Line.

This energetic switch from mobilization to immobilization leads to a critical consequence I cannot overstate. All cultural structures—from religious dicta to laws enforced by justice systems (with their underlying enforcement structure of escalating punishment), to educational systems, to family discipline—are built from and sustained by this domination/submission pairing. Hierarchy through mobilized dominators and immobilized submitters keeps our entire culture operating. And our conditioning from infancy to adulthood is one long internalization of these cultural structures. All states from Frozen Fear on down the vertical line reflect the human ability to internalize others' domination and keep those dicta going without the dominator present.

Clearly, we need social order. But if we don't understand the energetics that exist below the surface, we end up getting trapped in those dynamics. We confuse our state with what triggered it and then believe our internal narrative generated from that state. For example, someone who practices Catholicism might believe they are truly a sinner, rather than simply experience their anger, fear, guilt, and shame as transient energies moving through their body. Or, someone in an abusive relationship might see themselves as "bad" rather than recognize that they're in a collapsed immobilized response. Once we've identified with these states, we really have only two choices: suffer with them or endeavor to make them go away. We might try self-medication, therapy, or blame, all of which keep us swirling around in the original narrative.

Now that you understand the physiology of hierarchy, you can exercise this empowering and effective strategy for escaping the domination/submission game: First notice the relationship or circumstance that triggered your state. Then locate yourself on the Inner Map, and use your inner voice to sort through what happened according to the function of the state, something like, "Oh, I'm now in Frozen Fear, and I'm looking for an alpha to tell me what to do. This is a good time to shift my physiology." Or, "I've collapsed my body so as not to provoke my partner's rage. If I straighten my spine and pull my shoulders back, then I can feel what I am really feeling."

Overall, while our individualistic society tends to view Frozen Fear, Sadness, Despair, Guilt, and Shame as experiences unto themselves, I see them as outcomes of hierarchical dynamics. Trying to help someone move out of these immobilized states makes little sense, then, if those power dynamics aren't recognized.

While in immobilized states, people act predictably. They make agreements they won't keep (because their low status keeps them in a cycle of preserving their relationship by doing what they don't want to do); they stonewall (because their speech centers are somewhat disabled by their reactivity); they withdraw (because direct action will threaten the alpha); and they don't express anger or say what they really want (for the same reason).

Of course, immobilized states interlock with mobilized states, triggering predictable patterns in those in the dominator role as well. People in Pride or Anger feel chronic irritability with their "irresponsible" partner (the one making bad agreements); they're critical and judgmental, willingly going on the attack; they express anger but not fear and sadness. Someone in a mobilized state seems controlling and parental, while someone in an immobilized state seems weak and childlike. These interlocks can become a self-perpetuating cycle of ever-tightening knots of power struggle. No wonder relationships can be so incredibly frustrating.[9]

---

9 For more on how interlocking power dynamics work, see Chapter 8 of my book *The Relationship Ride: A Usable, Unusual, Transformative Guide* (Boulder, CO: Integrity Arts Press, 2012).

FROZEN FEAR

> *"Oh, my sweet summer child,"* Old Nan said quietly, *"what do you know of fear? Fear is for the winter, my little lord, when the snows fall a hundred feet deep and the ice wind comes howling out of the north. Fear is for the long night, when the sun hides its face for years at a time, and little children are born and live and die all in darkness while the direwolves grow gaunt and hungry, and the white walkers move through the woods."*[10]
> ~ George R.R. Martin

The function of Frozen Fear is to stop forward movement so as to orient to and assess threat, and to find and obey the alpha.

Frozen Fear is recognizable in our body as the "deer in the headlights" response. It can be difficult to observe in our fellow humans because we tend to judge someone as obstinate or aloof or rude when they stop speaking mid-conversation, rather than see through those responses to the Frozen Fear generating them. You know you're in Frozen Fear when your facial expression freezes, your heart pounds, and your body doesn't want to move. What may seem from the outside as "cool" is actually experienced inside as terror. Your speech tends to stop, as you focus only on monitoring the perceived threat and looking for external signals so you can choose your next action.

There is a dramatic cognitive shift from Agitated Fear to Frozen Fear. While someone in Agitated Fear still has enough clarity in their thinking to escape, the thoughts and speech of someone in Frozen Fear shut down because all attention is put on sorting out the perceived threat, which is apparently no longer escapable. True (though transient) cognitive disability has hit the brain, as the body's singular focus is on not being killed.[11]

Let's see what our sample people are thinking when they're in Frozen Fear:

---

10 George R.R. Martin, *A Game of Thrones* (New York: Bantam Books, 1996), p. 202.
11 This quality of Frozen Fear is what explains how difficult it can be to rouse oneself to take action in the face of a disaster.

Person #1 (self-esteem):
If I don't leave the house, maybe I'll be okay. But now that I'm home, I feel pretty awful. Maybe if I watch Netflix, I'll feel better. But I should be getting up and getting out. But I can't. So I'll just sit here. What show can I binge-watch?

Person #2 (climate change):
What do I do? I'll recycle. But China doesn't take recycling anymore! So I won't recycle. But I can't just throw all this plastic away. Oh, geez. I'll leave it right here. I can't decide. Do I still have time to walk to the meeting? I don't think I'll make it. But I can't drive; that's going to increase my carbon footprint. Where's my phone? I'll look at Facebook.

SADNESS

> *Beautiful things grow to a certain height and then they fall and fade off, breathing out memories as they decay.*[12]
> ~F. Scott Fitzgerald

The function of Sadness is to protest the loss of valued connection and create reconnection.

Sadness is clearly relational: consider a crying baby, almost impossible to not pick up and comfort. We associate Sadness with grief, though I'd argue that the impulse to cry retains a sense of agency that disappears with actual grief. With grief, we are coping with the loss; with Sadness, there is still energy coming from us to protest and thus potentially draw the loved one back in, undoing the loss. However, I classify Sadness as an immobilization response because the body wants to collapse and pull in.

In fact, the collapse of Sadness is a submission signal to the alpha, broadcasting the removal of threat while still communicating the protest of crying. (With couples in conflict, power struggles often stop when one person collapses into crying; the struggle is over because one has submitted to the other.) You know you're in Sadness when you feel a heaviness in your heart and a lump in your throat, a sense of being on

---

12 F. Scott Fitzgerald, *The Beautiful and Damned* (Mineola, NY: Dover Publications, Inc., 2019), p. 110.

the verge of crying. You may be frowning, knitting your eyebrows, and furrowing your forehead. Your thinking is slowed, preoccupied with retrieving the lost connection, which may be why your speech drags, sounding heavy and monotonous.

Here's what our sample people are thinking when they're in Sadness:

Person #1 (self-esteem):
I am so lonely. Where is everyone? Why have they left me?

Person #2 (climate change):
The polar bears have nothing to eat, and their ice floes are melting. So many species have gone extinct. The glaciers are melting off. The world will never be the same.

DESPAIR

> *My life is a perfect graveyard of buried hopes.*[13]
> ~L.M. Montgomery

The function of Despair is to abandon protest about lost connection as the body shuts down in its initial preparation for death.

Despair is what we typically view as depression. The lethargy, the thoughts about giving up on life, the need to pull away from external demands and be alone—these are emblematic mammalian responses to being separated from one's love object.[14]

Knowing what happens physiologically to a mammal that has been separated from a loved one explains how difficult it is for a human to tolerate Despair. Their immune system loses effectiveness; their heart-rate variability (an indicator of health) goes way down; they want to curl up and barely move. Basically, they've followed nature's law of economy: faced with the catastrophic loss of their caretaker, they've stopped expending the energy of protest. To be clear, the energy hasn't gone somewhere else; they've simply immobilized their sadness to conserve energy.

---
13 L.M. Montgomery, *Anne of Green Gables* (New York: Modern Library, 2008), p. 37.
14 Thomas Lewis, M.D., Fari Amini, M.D., Richard Lannon, M.D., *A General Theory of Love* (New York: Random House, 2000), pp. 76–91.

You know you're in Despair when your body is collapsed, as you pull in to save precious resources. Your facial expressions are static, and you may be unwilling to speak. Your thoughts are very slow, and your mood is one of hopelessness and resignation.

Let's check in with what our sample people are thinking when they're in Despair:

Person #1 (self-esteem):
I give up. No one cares about me. I'm all alone, and that will never change.

Person #2 (climate change):
We're in the sixth mass extinction. We're screwed. Humanity, the planet—it's all going to go. Nothing we do matters. Nothing I do matters. There's no point.

GUILT

Every man is guilty of all the good he did not do.[15]
~Voltaire

The function of Guilt is to immobilize one's own impulses so as to regain the alpha's good graces (and, in turn, access to the alpha's resources) and to avoid the loss and negative "correction" from the alpha or their lieutenants.

In Guilt, the energy that was expressed outwardly as aggression in Pride and Anger is now directed internally so as not to threaten the alpha. The energetic switch out of dominance and into submission that happened in Frozen Fear is now intensified, as the fear of retribution by the alpha keeps the stream of angry energy focused inward.

Our use of language to anchor into a certain state is particularly obvious at the level of Guilt and the level below it, Shame. This far Below The Line, we don't need an alpha threatening us in order to submit. Guilt, the combination of fear (of the alpha's retribution) and anger (that we don't get to do exactly what we want), means *we submit to others through our thoughts*. The religious dogma and moral codes of our socialization have

---

15 Voltaire, *The Age of Louis XIV* (*Le Siècle de Louis XIV*) (1751).

laid the tracks for us to follow externally imposed rules even when we're alone. When we don't follow our culture's principles, Guilt (and its more toxic cousin, Shame) will arise to try to refreeze us into submission. All mammals feel guilt, but we humans are brilliant at generating it.

You know you're in Guilt when you're sullen and silently resentful, as your hidden aggression is directed internally. Your speech is slow and difficult to hear. Your thoughts focus on your wrongdoing and the possible consequences, with some desperation about regaining the alpha's approval. Your posture is collapsed from your continued immobilization.[16]

Here's what our sample people are thinking when they're in Guilt:

Person #1 (self-esteem):
Oh, no! I said the wrong thing. That probably really hurt his feelings. What was I thinking? I have to apologize. That was so stupid of me! What have I done?

Person #2 (climate change):
As a part of humanity, I am responsible for ruining this beautiful planet. What have we done? I can't stand that I've contributed to all of this. We all deserve to be punished for what we've done!

SHAME

The shame that tormented me was all the more corrosive for having no very clear origin: I didn't know why I felt so tainted, and worthless, and wrong—only that I did, and whenever I looked up from my books I was swamped by slimy waters rushing in from all sides.[17]
~Donna Tartt

The function of Shame is to energetically freeze self-expression (anger, sadness, and fear, as well as sexual and joyful energies) in order to ward off aggression and/or loss of the alpha.

Shame is the result of the contempt of the dominator. It is the ultimate shutoff of personal power, the freezing of all impulses of self. Its

---

16 In fact, when I see clients who are caught in Guilt and Shame, I ask them to straighten up so that their solar plexus is pressed out instead of caved in. This simple physical shift allows them to access the anger that their collapse has kept them disconnected from. I describe Guilt and Shame as "pulling out the power cord"; straightening up plugs it back in.
17 Donna Tartt, *The Goldfinch* (New York: Little, Brown and Company, 2013), p. 392.

hallmark, self-hatred, is internalized aggression—the energy that cannot be externally expressed because of the high threat of retribution from the alpha. Instead, that energy is aimed directly at annihilating the self so as to reduce that threat.

You know you're in Shame when your shoulders are turned in an intense effort to further collapse your body. Your eyes are downcast, your face is drawn, and your speech is labored, often nonexistent, as you have scant bandwidth to pay attention to what's going on outside of you. While your external cues suggest inertness, internally there is a cascade of energy, with self-aggressive thoughts predominating and an eye on restoring your dominator's approval.

It's harder to listen to what our sample folks are thinking when in Shame, isn't it?

Person #1 (self-esteem):
I hate myself. I should die. I am bad to the core, defective, worthless. I deserve to be crushed.

Person #2 (climate change):
Humans are bad; I'm a human. We've ruined everything. We suck. I suck. I hope we all perish. The world will do just fine without us.

Climbing Down Through Reactive Brain

Let's recap what happens as we move down the vertical line, from Pride to Anger all the way to Shame. With each state, there is progressively less movement of energy. In Pride, we feel very energized, even powerful (though I don't consider this "real" power, as it will inevitably be thwarted by the resistance of those submitting to us). We don't question ourselves when we're in Pride (because of the risk of plummeting to Shame). This explains our rigidity and the difficulty of getting along with us while we're in Pride or Anger, as we rarely see ourselves as the source of issues in our relationships.

In Anger, we feel quite energized, though we may start to see the relational costs of our aggression (if we can notice how we're scaring people into submission and how they're moving away from us). Agitated Fear can still feel good, if we successfully get away from the threat, but our cultural stories of cowardice infringe on our sense of power. In the switchover state of Frozen Fear, we no longer feel powerful, as our physiology is immobilizing us into submission. But there's still lots of energy under the surface, energy we can use if we move back up to Agitated Fear.

In Sadness, we've begun an inner collapse, though there is still energy in crying and trying to elicit a response from a loved one. In Despair, energy is blocked even more in the collapse of finally giving up on trying to get the loved one to respond. In Guilt, we've turned ourselves inside out enough that we use the stifled aggression to keep our impulses at bay the way we were taught to.

Finally, in Shame, we want to pull in and freeze any self-expression at all, to become invisible. There is the least apparent energy in Shame, which is why it is situated closest to Death on the Inner Map. The energy isn't gone, though; it's simply redirected. The aggressive energy that can't be expressed towards the overpowering alpha gets aimed at stopping self-expression (not just one's behaviors, as in Guilt). Fear of humiliation submerges the real self. That self hasn't disappeared, however. With the right trigger, self-expression will inevitably, and often unpredictably, spring to the surface.

It may be quite clear by now that all of the states Below The Line—most notably Shame—are social constructs. While many great thinkers[18] walk us through the minefield of shame and vulnerability as real experiences that must be processed so as not to pull us down into those states, I don't view Shame this way. I see Shame as a temporary state of submission resulting from aggression and contempt from someone in Pride or Anger. Of course, Shame is typically experienced as much more than that because of the human proclivity to tell stories about it ("I am bad! I am worthless. Because I am bad and worthless, I must die!"). We have no idea that we're reacting as all mammals do, collapsing—from Frozen Fear down to Shame—to submit to a dominator. Because we've internalized the stories we've heard over and over (starting with the crux of the Shame

---

18 Brené Brown is the first who comes to mind.

story, Original Sin), most of us are walking around as Shame triggers, waiting to be shamed.

Phew! Are you still with me? If you're exhausted by just reading through the different states of Reactive Brain, you're getting a sense of the cost of living in it. Remember that Reactive Brain emotions are "negative" only because they use up energy. And they use up energy because reactivity elicits stress chemicals. All of Reactive Brain exists in a field of resistance because keeping hierarchy in place—through domination and submission, mobilization and immobilization—necessarily generates resistance. Even though humans dominate and submit all the livelong day, no one wants to be controlled in an ongoing way. Every push leads to a push back. We'll give up the self temporarily, but over time, suppressing one's self is like trying to keep a beach ball underwater: it takes a lot of energy, and when it finally emerges, it will blast forth.

Chapter 3

Functions of Levels of Consciousness: Creative Brain

Before we cross The Line into Creative Brain, let's take a moment to look at what the action of crossing over actually means.

In *Power vs. Force*, Hawkins emphasizes that moving out of Force (here, Reactive Brain) into Power (here, Creative Brain) is a huge shift in consciousness. By taking this step, we are instantly transported from a world where we are "at the effect of" to one where we increasingly understand that we are the source of our reality. Embodying this concept will transform your life. Once you see how changing your state changes the actual reality you're living in, you'll know what true power is. Far from the resistance-filled experience of Reactive Brain, crossing The Line means you're stepping into a world where your intentions are supported, you live in flow, and you are actively collaborating with the universe.

Hawkins believes that courage is the elemental force that allows one to cross over this crucial bridge. While I agree with this, I propose an even more important quality: willingness. To live from Creative Brain, we must be willing to give up every story—personal, familial, cultural—learned from Reactive Brain. To release the ego's tentacled grip on old stories, we must leap into territories uncharted by our species' best thinkers, storytellers, and myth makers. We humans have accrued seemingly inexhaustible evidence that our survival is threatened, and that our best offense is a strong defense. As we face into the current calamities of climate change and potential mass extinction, we may feel an even stronger pull to believe that we must battle each other, and our very humanness, to ensure the survival of life itself. Now is the time to firmly commit to telling generative narratives that anchor us into states Above The Line, where we dwell in our natural creativity and easily connect with each other and nature itself, allowing access to infinite new possibilities for healing ourselves and our precious planet.

As you certainly understand by now, Creative Brain is an entirely different land from Reactive Brain. Freed from the bondage of stress chemicals and unconstructive thoughts and emotions, you can now relax and open to innovative thinking and fresh experiences. You can instantly connect with your internal self and tune in to what you really want. Your relationships will immediately shift: those whom you viewed as enemies can now take their rightful place as allies. Power struggles stop on a dime, replaced by collaboration and co-creation. Intimacy deepens. Your Reactive Brain's perception of a hostile world is replaced by a strong sense of a friendly universe you belong in and to.[1]

Even more important, this shift into Creative Brain changes the energetic field you exist in. You are leaving behind the field of resistance and entering into energetic flow. And, as you progress Above The Line (from Neutrality to Acceptance to Appreciation on up to Peace), your consciousness increasingly expands and you gain more power to manifest what you really want. Stepping across The Line, you lose your ego and gain an ever-increasing capacity to create the life you're here to live.

As you navigate Creative Brain, you'll discover that, though its increasingly expanded levels of consciousness seem to blur together into simply feeling good, each has a particular function that supports who we are as humans. As with Reactive Brain, all mammals are capable of experiencing every state; in fact, non-human mammals are in Creative Brain most of the time because, without human language to anchor into states through stories, they quickly move through their contracted reactions to perceived threat, back to expansiveness.[2] (This is why it can be so relaxing to hang out with non-human animals.)

Willingness. It offers a passageway through the darkness of the views of

---

[1] When asked what the most vital question facing humanity is, Albert Einstein answered, "Is the universe friendly?" Source: Irving Oyle, *The New American Medicine Show* (Santa Cruz, CA: Unity Press, 1979), p. 163.

[2] Les Fehmi, Ph.D., and Jim Robbins, *The Open-Focus Brain: Harnessing the Power of Attention to Heal Mind and Body* (Boston: Trumpeter Books, 2007), p. 14.

Reactive Brain. Are you willing to give up everything you've believed in order to step into a reality that you've never known, perhaps never even heard of? Are you willing to give up your survival fears, to let go of their grip, to yield to energies you can't see but can access the full power of?

Are you?

Then let's cross The Line.

NEUTRALITY

Praise be to God I'm not good, / And have the natural egotism of flowers / And rivers following their bed / Preoccupied without knowing it / Only with blooming and flowing. / This is the only mission in the World, / This—to exist clearly, / And to know how to do it without thinking about it.[3]
~Fernando Pessoa

The function of Neutrality is to face into what is.

In Neutrality, facing into what is happening in the here and now moves us out of denial (what classical psychodynamic theory rates as a "primitive" defense) and into the flow of reality. Neutrality brings us into the moment, to what truly is. "It is what it is" is the main, perhaps only, narrative of this state. Being willing to navigate the "is-ness" of life is the first step out of the field of resistance of Reactive Brain and into the flow of Creative Brain.[4]

The human propensity for denial is impressive and actually fairly functional. Without it, we might never step into, let alone drive, a two-ton vehicle that can instantly become a death machine. But *denying reality means staying out of the flow of the energy of creation.* By not facing into what is, we don't slow down to process difficult emotions. Avoiding them might feel better, but it costs us feedback that would actually reorient us to reality.

You know you're in Neutrality when you turn back towards experiencing what really is happening, in and around you. Your face may wince at what you're now letting yourself see, but, with breath and attention, you can process your unwanted feelings still present from Reactive Brain, thereby relaxing your body and slowing your pulse. After the first surge

---
3 Fernando Pessoa, *The Keeper of Sheep* (Sheep Meadow Press, 1997, originally 1925).
4 Note that most popular media exist Below The Line, with an emphasis on "it shouldn't be this way." Read practically any newspaper article and you'll feel the toxicity of Reactive Brain in its dramatic storytelling about someone who is to blame for making untenable conditions for someone else.

of previously unfelt emotional energy passes through, you feel an internal opening. Your thoughts calm down and reflect this shift in their "is-ness."

Let's catch up with our two sample people to find out what they're thinking, now that they've stepped over The Line, into Neutrality:

Person #1 (self-esteem):
I am what I am.

Person #2 (climate change):
It is what it is.

ACCEPTANCE

For after all, the best thing one can do / When it is raining, is let it rain.[5]
~Henry Wadsworth Longfellow

The function of Acceptance is to accept what is.

Acceptance—saying "yes" to reality as it is, in the here and now—is the next step to expanding our consciousness as we move up the vertical line. It is not enough to move out of denial into facing what is. To completely come into flow, we must *accept* what is.

Imagine life as a running river. Denial (not a river in Eqypt, for sure) is not seeing the river. Neutrality says, "Oh, there's a river!" Acceptance brings us closer to the energy of the river: "I accept the river-ness of this body of water. It has properties of a river—water and current, a riverbed and banks. I am willing to interact with the river as it is."

Accepting what is doesn't mean giving up. The opposite is true. When we can be with reality as it comes to us, we are able to see clearly and then choose authentic, appropriate action. And we have more fuel to act because we are no longer using our energetic resources to try to make that reality different from what it is.

While acceptance may sound simple, we're all familiar with these non-

---

5 Henry Wadsworth Longfellow, *Tales of a Wayside Inn* (1863).

accepting statements:

- It shouldn't be that way.
- I can't believe I/you/they did that.
- People shouldn't act like that.
- That shouldn't have happened.
- I shouldn't have said/done that.
- My body/habits/thoughts/life should be different.

Practice noticing when you think these sorts of thoughts (or hear others say them). Stop. Take a breath. First respond with Neutrality ("Yes, and it is what it is."), then move to Acceptance ("I accept that this is what is happening.").

You know you're in Acceptance when your breathing is slowed down. Your body is more relaxed: your shoulders drop and move back, and tension drains from your face as your jaw loosens its clamped-down resistance. Your eyes can focus on what is actually in front of them. Your thoughts are more expanded, with new possibilities emerging on the horizon.

Here's what our sample people are thinking when they're in Acceptance:

Person #1 (self-esteem):
I accept all of who I am and all of what I've done.

Person #2 (climate change):
Today, I accept everything that is happening, all that has happened, and all that will happen.

APPRECIATION

I wonder if the snow loves the trees and fields, that it kisses them so gently? And then it covers them up snug, you know, with a white quilt; and perhaps it says, "Go to sleep, darlings, till the summer comes again."[6]
~Lewis Carroll

The function of Appreciation is to orient to the positive qualities of what is.

Appreciation connects us to an even more powerful energy of reality than Acceptance does. *What we appreciate appreciates.*[7] That is, our appreciative attention itself increases the value of whatever we're appreciating. Even more important, as we choose Appreciation, we ourselves are filled with expanding energy.

You don't have to feel appreciative to appreciate. As with all of the states on the Inner Map, simply speaking the narrative can generate the state. I have generated the state of Appreciation by simply deciding to appreciate whatever is around me, from asphalt to stoplights to the metal chair I'm sitting on right now (it feels stable and cool underneath me).

You know you're in Appreciation when the relaxation that begins in Neutrality and Acceptance transforms into a bubbling-up of energy with each new thought. Your body experiences a wonderful combination of ease and aliveness. Your face is even more open, as positivity becomes its own reward, activating "attractor energies" (described in the Introduction) to pull in positive responses from others. Your appreciative thoughts lead to the discovery of more and more things to appreciate, creating an ever-expanding chain of well-being.

Let's see what our sample people are thinking when they're in Appreciation:

---

6 Lewis Carroll, *Alice's Adventures in Wonderland & Through the Looking-Glass* (New York: Bantam Dell, 1984), p. 117.
7 Kathlyn Hendricks, personal communication, 2000.

Person #1 (self-esteem):
I appreciate myself for showing up, doing my best every day. I appreciate all of those around me. I appreciate asphalt!

Person #2 (climate change):
I appreciate our beautiful, amazing planet. I appreciate everyone who is stepping in to change who we've been as humans. I appreciate nature and how we can co-create with its energies!

LOVE

> *[T]he best and most beautiful things in the world cannot be seen nor even touched, but just felt in the heart.*[8]
> ~Helen Keller

The function of Love is to join with the energy of the universe to co-create.

Love conquers all. Love is the answer. All we need is love. Philosophers, poets, and songwriters have always understood that Love is a magnificent life-force, far beyond simple romantic love and the miracle of human procreation it can lead to.

Love is a huge energy field, inside of which we are capable of miraculous feats. At the level of Love, we can access the power of healing for ourselves and others; we are willing to take on difficult or daunting tasks; we have the courage to step into imminent danger with grace and strength.

Choosing Love takes us into a realm filled with unprecedented power. Every major religion integrates this idea into its teachings, universally directing us to love our neighbors as ourselves. Living from Love means letting go of our judgments about everyone and everything around us. Every time we think about someone or something we love easily, we connect to a flow of highly charged, transformative energy.[9]

---

[8] Letter dated June 8, 1891, from Helen Keller, at age ten, to the Reverend Phillips Brooks, in Helen Keller, *The Story of My Life* (1905).
[9] For more about a highly effective process for generating love, see Gay Hendricks, Ph.D., *Learning to Love Yourself: A Guide to Becoming Centered* (New Jersey: Prentice Hall, 1982).

You know you're in Love when your body is even more expanded than in Neutrality, Acceptance, and Appreciation. Your heart feels warm and open; your chest expands; your face is bright, smiling. Your thoughts are focused on the object of your love and expand to encompass more and more of the world—which may be why you feel on top of it!

Here's what our sample people are thinking when they're in Love:

Person #1 (self-esteem):
I love every cell of my being, as I love every cell of all beings.

Person #2 (climate change):
I love all that is. I co-create with all that is.

A Note About "Upper Limits"

As you keep moving up the vertical line, how are you doing? Have you noticed the challenge of embodying increasingly expanded energy? If so, you may be encountering what Gay and Kathlyn Hendricks call the "Upper Limit Problem,"[10] the difficulty we humans have in feeling good for more than a few seconds at a time. As a species, we've mastered the states Below The Line; the realms Above The Line are giving us brand-new challenges, as we learn to embody feeling good, *really* good, even wonderful!

---

10 Gay Hendricks, Ph.D., and Kathlyn Hendricks, Ph.D., *Conscious Loving: The Journey to Co-Commitment* (New York: Bantam Books, 1990).

JOY

We are not going to change the whole world, but we can change ourselves and feel free as birds. We can be serene even in the midst of calamities and, by our serenity, make others more tranquil. Serenity is contagious. If we smile at someone, he or she will smile back. And a smile costs nothing. We should plague everyone with joy. If we are to die in a minute, why not die happily, laughing?[11]
~Sri Swami Satchidananda

The function of Joy is to celebrate life.

Joy bubbles. It's effervescent. It can be quietly expansive or fist-pumping, dancing-around energized. All of this extra pizzazz coursing through the body is the increased energy from having moved beyond even Love. Hooking into Joy is like plugging our energy cord into the flow of life. We're connected to the natural energy of the universe!

Great avatars, like the Dalai Lama, Archbishop Desmond Tutu, and Gurumayi (Chidvilasananda), have clearly mastered Joy. Even during a serious public talk, they naturally hang out in Joy, easily chuckling at our human foibles and the absurdities of life.

As you savor Joy right now, notice that your body may not be able to contain it. By this level of consciousness, your body probably needs practice holding high vibrations to be able to feel Joy for longer than a few seconds.

Here's what our sample people are thinking when they're in Joy:

Person #1 (self-esteem):
I breathe into my body and feel every cell dancing! I laugh and laugh and dance and sing at every opportunity!

Person #2 (climate change):
I celebrate life and all that is!

---

[11] Sri Swami Satchidananda, *The Yoga Sutras of Patanjali* (Buckingham, VA: Integral Yoga Publications, 1978), pp. 136–37.

PEACE

> *You may say I'm a dreamer / But I'm not the only one. /*
> *I hope someday you'll join us / And the world will live as one.*[12]
> ~John Lennon

The function of Peace is to exist as one with all that is.

Peace. We've made our way to the top of the Inner Map[13], to the most expanded state, carrying the most energy and thus the most power. We humans talk, write, and dream about Peace. *Let there be peace on earth. Peace be with you. Visualize world peace.* As the highest state, it can seem remote, even unobtainable. It is, after all, about unity with the cosmos.

Some meditate many hours a day to ground their knowledge and experience of the unity of all that is. Others seek Peace through psychedelics, blissing out as they watch everything vibrating around them. No wonder it is so difficult for us to generate even a temporary state of Peace in our daily life, let alone in a whole world of 7.8 billion lives.

You know you're in Peace when your body is so relaxed that you are no longer aware of your own outline. Your face and body emit a glow that others notice, but they can't put their finger on what they're perceiving. Others are drawn to being with you, relishing the exquisiteness of the vibration they can feel from you. Your consciousness blends with the consciousness of the universe: you can perceive the energy of all that is as you lose your sense of separation from any of it.

Let's check in with what our two sample people are thinking, now that they're finally in Peace:

---

12 John Lennon and Yoko Ono, "Imagine" (London: Apple Records, 1971).
13 Note that Hawkins' Map of Consciousness® goes beyond Peace to Enlightenment. I've decided to take my map only as high as I understand; someday I'll create the Inner Map II.

Person #1 (self-esteem):
I connect to all that is. I am one with all that is. I am a divine being of love and light. All is well.

Person #2 (climate change):
I connect to all that is. I am one with all that is. I am part of nature, and so I—and all humans—co-create with nature. All is well.

Wow! Do you feel as enlivened as I do, simply walking through the different states of Creative Brain? Tune in to your renewed sense of vitality, the expansive experience of your body, how your mind has opened to possibilities. It's as if a portal to the infinite has opened, connecting you to all that is.

Feel your way around this other realm, the one Above The Line, the field of no resistance. This is what flow feels like; here is where life is easy, serendipity is common, and co-creativity is the name of the game. As you anchor yourself to what is most essential about you, about others, and about the world, know that you've discovered the place where your real, evolutionary power exists. And the best part? *You yourself created it.*

Chapter 4

Navigating the Inner Map

You've been learning lots of concepts that may seem abstract right now. Let's see how they play out when practically applied to everyday life. Each of the following exercises[1] is designed to shift your state out of Reactive Brain and into Creative Brain. (To master every state, you can even use these to shift from Above The Line to Below The Line.)

Remember, all energies are part of our mammalian functioning. As you become more skillful at changing your state, you'll notice that you are just like a radio. Many signals are broadcasting simultaneously through the atmosphere. The question is, which signal, which frequency of energy, do you want to tune in to?

Exercise: Self-Hypnotic Induction

To the human brain, imagining an experience can be as powerful as actually having it. Our thoughts, then, are often highly effective, albeit generally unconscious, hypnotic inductions. Repetitive thoughts, along with any sensory details and allusions to particular memories we've added in, generate certain states in ourselves. These states, in turn, move us towards particular outcomes. In other words, we're our own hypnotherapists, though we're often hypnotizing ourselves into states Below The Line. I believe that almost all of us are highly skilled, albeit unconsciously, at hypnotizing ourselves, and that this ability explains a great deal of mental illness.

For example, a client[2] came in who was very frightened of flying. When I asked them what they thought when they thought about flying, they said, "Well, I think about the door closing and how I can't get out and

---
1 You can download PDFs of these exercises at www.JuliaColwell.com/Books, so that you can print them out and write on them.
2 All client details are a composite.

we'll be flying for hours and I CAN'T GET OUT. So I start to feel panicky and my heart races and I can't BREATHE because it's so stuffy. So I watch the door and think about pounding on it and still I CAN'T GET OUT! So, yeah, I never want to fly again."

See the skill involved in this storytelling?

I asked the client to come up with a new story. It sounded something like this: "I settle into my seat and look around at all the friendly people. I feel cozy and happy. I take out my journal and write about how much I appreciate the fluffiness of clouds, while I sip on my tasty drink, occasionally looking out the window at the deep blue sky."

Want to try it? Here you'll intentionally induce a state Above The Line, but this process is particularly useful for interrupting yourself when you've induced a state Below The Line.

A powerful hypnotic induction requires a relaxed state and sensory details and imagery that fit the person being hypnotized. To induce a particular state:

- Look at the Inner Map, notice where you are located on it, and decide which state Above The Line you want to induce.

- Write down memories and any other images that reflect this state, focusing on their sensory details: What did you see? hear? smell? taste? touch?

- On a recording device, speaking slowly, describe these memories and images with as many details as possible that are specific to the state you want to induce.

- Sit or lie down in a comfortable position with your eyes closed. Breathing slowly and deeply, play the recording, and place your awareness on your body sensations.

- Open your eyes. Take time to reorient to your current reality while bringing that state of consciousness to your here and now. That is, if you're inducing Neutrality, what "is-ness" can you face into? If Acceptance, what can you accept in your life right now? If

Appreciation or Love, what and whom can you appreciate or love? If Joy or Peace, what in your life can you feel joyful or peaceful about?

Here's an example of how and when to use Self-Hypnotic Induction. Perhaps you've been watching the news or talking to friends about the state of the world. You notice you don't feel very good and realize you're in Reactive Brain. You take a few minutes to tune in to the story you've been playing out in your mind, something like, "Oh, geez! I heard that new statistic about the amount of plastic in the oceans. How terrible!" You take out your Inner Map and see that you're at Despair. You decide to change your state to Appreciation. You recall an experience you had on a beach, since the ocean is on your mind, and you write it down:

> There I was on the beach, walking along, noticing the difference between the hot sand and the cool water rushing between my toes. I hear the waves crashing nearby and the seagulls crying overhead. I take a deep breath, smelling the salty air. I look far out to sea, feeling my whole body relaxing deeply as I take in the beauty of the endless horizon and the billowing clouds. As I notice each of these details, I well up with a deep sense of appreciation for all that life has brought my way. I imagine the myriad ways I am supported by life, from the food I ate today to the air I am breathing, to the love I've felt through my life. I look around and my heart swells with all the gifts that are mine.

You get your phone out and record what you wrote, then lie down and get comfortable while listening to the recording. (By the way, this exercise won't solve the initial problem of the plastic-laden ocean, but it likely will give you energy to take a proactive step that expresses Appreciation.)

Exercise: I Choose Happy! Process

A few years ago, I was in the doldrums. I had visions for my life and my career, and I kept missing the mark. So I did what I do at such times: I took a dream day, which is when I take lots of space to journal, draw, paint, and do whatever I can to move out of my ordinary reality into one more expanded.

Early in that day, I started thinking about the iconic spiritual question "Would you rather be right or happy?" Having asked myself this countless times over the years, I'd grown accustomed to the flow that happens in my relationship when I stop insisting on my expectations of my partner and tilt over into the territory of "happy." But I hadn't applied this question to life overall. What if I was creating my own suffering by trying to force my ideas of what my life should look like rather than allowing it to unfold?

In retrospect, applying this spiritual question generally is quite obvious. At the time, however, my eyes were opened to the wonder of what had been actually happening right in front of me all along. The I Choose Happy! Process was born.

This exercise should take about an hour to do, and will set you up for the next exercise, Writing Your Manifesto.

1. Generate a clear commitment to feeling happy over being right. When I present this step to groups, someone inevitably says, "Well, I'm happy being right!" Go ahead; say it out loud, even if it sounds corny to your ears: "I commit to feeling happy over being right."

2. Define your Measures of Success (MOS). In other words, how do you know whether you're having a successful life or not?

    a. List all of your current MOS.

    When I did this process with a client, their list looked something like this:

    - Make a lot of money

    - Have a great (meaning skinny) body

    - Get an advanced degree

    - Have a nice car

    - Be married

    - Have kids

    - Be famous

b. Next to each item, list whose idea it is, that is, where did it come from? Note whether any of them are *your* MOS.

   Now my client's list looked like this:

   - Make a lot of money: THE US CULTURE
   - Have a great body: THE US CULTURE
   - Get an advanced degree: MY PATERNAL GRANDFATHER
   - Have a nice car: THE US CULTURE
   - Be married: MY MOTHER
   - Have kids: MY MOTHER
   - Be famous: THE US CULTURE

Now that it's clear that your MOS mostly reflect what you've learned from other people, let's find out what's authentic for you.

c. List your own MOS. Make this list as long and as detailed as possible.

   Here's an approximation of my client's list:

   - Sleep great
   - Feel calm
   - Be outside as much as possible
   - Feel connected to nature and my soul
   - Laugh
   - Play
   - Sing and make music every day
   - Savor wonderful food
   - Feel connected with and loving to my wife

- Move my body
- Be challenged intellectually
- Feel grateful for my existence
- Know I'm making a difference in people's lives

3. Now look back over your life, including what is happening now. List the results you have created and are creating that you LOVE. Star the ones you'd like to create even more of.

    This is such a rich inquiry. So often, our attention is focused on what is wrong with us, how we should be different or "improve." But, to survey all of the wonders we've created and to acknowledge who we've had to be to create them? Wow. Now, like gems that have been buried in the sand, the treasures of your life can be brushed off to shine.

    Here, again, is an approximation of my client's list:

    - Deep friendships
    - Great love with many partners (including my wife)
    - Amazing adventures that are fun to recount and reminisce about
    - So much beauty!
    - Special moments with a whole host of people
    - Lots of challenging, engaging work
    - Many moments of awe
    - Lots of times when I laughed until I cried
    - Connections with four-leggeds

    (When they went back through their list, they starred every item.)

4. Review your three lists. What do you now see about yourself? What are your values? Who are you really in the world?

My client wrote something like this:

> I walk around deeply loving people and being loved back. They trust me and I trust them. I see beauty everywhere and hear music even when no one is playing it. I feel awe in my connection with the world and play every chance I get.

Do you see what's happened? From the first list—by which my client had been judging themselves as a failure—to this statement of self, they were able to step back and feel confident in how they had been following their own path all along.

After my dream day, I felt that same fire. I'd discovered how I'd been anchored into an unseen force that had been guiding me, co-creating with me, all along.

Completing the Self-Hypnotic Induction and I Choose Happy! Process sets you up for this next, profoundly life-altering exercise.

Exercise: Writing Your Manifesto

A few years ago, I noticed a background thrum in my life, thoughts and beliefs that seemed to be an ongoing part of my awareness but that I didn't consciously know were there. If I tuned in, I'd hear—faint like the music track in an elevator—things like "A penny saved is a penny earned," or "You're born alone; you die alone." Clearly my conditioning had taken root. During darker times of my life, these underlying beliefs would take over my thoughts as I'd spin from "I can't do this," to "I'm too stupid," to "What's the point?" to "I should die." Eventually I realized that I had installed the thoughts I'd grown up with into my consciousness like malware.

I started using the Self-Hypnosis Induction and I Choose Happy! Process, a practice that eventually blossomed into one of the most powerful tools I've created: Writing Your Manifesto. I view my own manifesto as *me made manifest*. It's a living, evolving description of me from the most expanded level of consciousness I've been able to muster. It's clearly aspirational, and I strive every day to live into it. My favorite way to start the day is to stand in front of the kitchen window, raise my arms, and recite this to the birds:

> I am La-di-dah Star. I am a divine being of love and light. I've come to this planet to have a great time, have wonderful adventures, and to support the shift beyond hierarchy into co-creativity. I embody my divinity and am a mirror to all I meet of their most amazing beingness. I live from and in space and in the magical energy of flow. I move back and forth between space and form, and accompany others as they do the same.
>
> I love every bit of my being—as I love every bit of all beings—from the most expanded to the most contracted. I focus on strengthening my ability to love steadily, consistently, like a cascading river. As one cell of more than 7.8 billion others in the human body, I celebrate my role of thriving, expanding, and evolving, to serve myself and all of the galaxy.
>
> I live in a friendly universe. I trust myself, the world, and Source. I know that, as I live in impeccable integrity, life is sweeping me along my perfect path. I know that all is unfolding perfectly, and that all is well. I and those around me easily move out of old patterns into new possibilities. We playfully move out of Reactive Brain into Creative Brain, unleashing our gifts, power, and creativity.
>
> My inner peace is reflected by deep sleep, nourishing rest, deep contentment, wonderful dreams, and the ability to choose my most conscious response. I move out into the world with an open, loving heart, celebrating and appreciating the miracle of life and of my own existence, as I step into the flow of magic and the magic of flow.

What do you think? Are you interested in taking your self-hypnotic skills to the next level? Merriam-Webster defines "manifesto" as "a written statement declaring publicly the intentions, motives, or views of its issuer." Remember, your manifesto is your declaration of *YOU made manifest*. It describes who you are at your highest vibration; it is organic and fluid, revisable as you wish.

The point here is to give your mind a new story to *re-mind* yourself of! Over time, those old Reactive Brain stories of survival thrumming in the back of your consciousness will lose energy and ultimately dissipate, as your manifesto becomes the main story you tell yourself — no matter what.

Consider including these points in your manifesto:

- Your life purpose
- Archetypes that your life expresses
- Your most cherished values
- How you want to interact with yourself, the world, and Source
- Your intentions and commitments
- Your biggest aspirations for your life

After you write your manifesto, I recommend that you memorize it. Read it into a recording device and play it back so that you can get used to the words in your own voice. Repeat it to yourself, especially when you're in a relaxed and open state. Notice how this new story of YOU changes the way you talk to yourself and opens up new possibilities around you.

Exercise: Shift-and-Anchor Process

Way back in Chapter 1, I told you we'd get to a process that would include the elements you've learned in this book. To recap, you:

1. Identify your current state (and the story behind it).
2. Feel the feelings that triggered and sustain this state.
3. Choose the state you'd like to be in.
4. Anchor yourself into that state through a new, equally compelling narrative.

I access this process all day long. When I'm not feeling good, I'll realize I'm in Reactive Brain, then figure out what level I'm at. I might notice I'm in Agitated Fear, thinking something like, "Uh-oh, what's going to happen?! It's not going to turn out well." Deciding I want to shift, I'll move around, maybe wave my arms in the air and jump up and down (this makes for some strange looks at the coffee shop). I'll choose a state Above The Line that I want to inhabit. I'm a great fan of Appreciation, so I often choose to appreciate something, anything ("I love the rosette the barista makes on top of my latte.").

My clients are used to this process. They'll walk into my office and tell me the story they're stuck in, knowing they probably won't stay there for long. We identify the feelings behind the story, and they spend some time expressing: pushing on a wall, crying, maybe running around yelling, "FREAKOUT!" Once those dense energies are moved out, they decide what emotional state they want to feel, and tell a new story until they're at that level.

I've witnessed this process work its magic many times, from folks who were suicidally depressed, to people struggling in their relationships, to those experiencing debilitating anxiety. The power in Shift-and-Anchor is that it unplugs us from levels of consciousness that are dense and contracted (thus very low in energy and power) and moves us into states that are expanded, open, and full of life energy.

Read through the following steps of the Shift-and-Anchor Process; then I'll walk you through it with an example.

1. Write the 14 levels of consciousness on index cards, one per card: Shame, Guilt, Despair, Sadness, Frozen Fear, Agitated Fear, Anger, Pride, Neutrality, Acceptance, Appreciation, Love, Joy, Peace.

2. Spread the index cards around the room in order, from Shame to Peace. (Make a special demarcation at The Line so that you can see which levels are Below The Line and which are Above The Line.)

3. Describe the issue you want to address, using your whole body, exaggerating your voice and movements.

4. Still standing and moving, answer these questions:

- *What is my bottom-line story of this issue?*
- *Am I willing to shift?* If not, come back and do the process later.
- *What level of consciousness am I at with this issue?* Go stand by that level's card.

5. Play around with some shift moves, and notice your body expand:
   - Breathe
   - Dance
   - Laugh
   - Chant
   - Jump
   - Speak the unarguable truth—**S.E.W.**[3]:
     - *What body **sensations** am I having?*
     - *What **emotions** go with these sensations?*
     - *What do I really **want**?*

6. Decide if you've expanded as much as you want. If not, do more shift moves until your body feels sufficiently expanded. Answer this question: *What level of consciousness am I at now?* Go stand by that level's card.

7. Use your whole body to tell a new story that anchors you into this state.

8. Write your new story down; tell people around you. Really anchor it!

Let's see how these steps might look in practice. Because this is a body-centered process, it's worth taking the time to make the cards per step #1, spread them around the room per step #2, and physically move through the remaining steps—though you can still benefit from simply thinking through each step. It's all about what you're hypnotizing yourself into,

---

[3] You can find out much more about the S.E.W. process in my book *The Relationship Skills Workbook: A Do-It-Yourself Guide to a Thriving Relationship* (Boulder, CO: Sounds True, 2014).

right? Now, the remaining steps:

1. Describe the issue you want to address, using your whole body, exaggerating your voice and movements:

    Standing, jutting out your jaw, and making fists, you say, "I got a bad review at my job. I feel like crap, and I hate my stupid boss."

2. Still standing and moving, answer these questions:

    - *What is my bottom-line story of this issue?*

        "I hate my job!" As you move around, your story ends up at "I suck."

    - *Am I willing to shift?* If not, come back and do the process later.

        "Yes!"

    - *What level of consciousness am I at with this issue?* Go stand by that level's card.

        You've moved to Shame, having started at Anger.

3. Play around with some shift moves, and notice your body expand:

    - Breathe
    - Dance
    - Laugh
    - Chant
    - Jump
    - Speak the unarguable truth—**S.E.W.**:

        - *What body **sensations** am I having?*

            You feel a clutching in your solar plexus and an overall sense of collapse.

        - *What **emotions** go with these sensations?*

Mad: "I don't like going through this. And I didn't like that evaluation."

Scared: "I'm afraid of getting attacked if I show who I really am. And I'm afraid the evaluation was correct, that I'm over my head at my job."

Sad: "I feel sad that I haven't been myself lately. I miss me!"

- *What do I really **want**?*

    "I want to trust myself. I want to be big in the world. I want to fully express myself at work!"

4. Decide if you've expanded as much as you want. If not, do more shift moves until your body feels sufficiently expanded. Answer this question: *What level of consciousness am I at now?* Go stand by that level's card.

    You sense that you're now at Acceptance.

5. Use your whole body to tell a new story that anchors you into this state:

    "I accept myself; I accept my boss; I accept the circumstances of my job. I realize I've been afraid to speak up and say what I'm really thinking. Actually, I appreciate the opportunity to see all of this. I appreciate my boss for hanging in there with me and telling me the truth. And I appreciate myself for being strong enough to look at all of this!"

    Check it out! In the telling of your new story, you can further expand and shift your state, in this case, from Acceptance to Appreciation.

6. Write your new story down; tell people around you. Really anchor it!

Ready to try it?

Here's a powerful and touching example of this process, shared (with permission) by my beloved friend and colleague, Julia Munson. Julia is an experienced therapist who has been using the Inner Map with clients for the past few years. Here's her story:

The background to this session is that Laura, age 32, was diagnosed in the summer of 2018 with stage III ovarian cancer. Laura had just graduated with her master's degree that May and was looking forward to both launching her career and starting a family with her husband, Brad.

Instead, in September, Laura had major surgery that removed her ovaries, fallopian tubes, uterus, and cervix. The surgeons also removed her spleen, appendix, gallbladder, omentum, and part of her colon, stripped her bladder, and removed 25 lymph nodes from various locations (20 were positive for cancer). The surgery was followed by six rounds of chemo.

I was in touch with Laura off and on throughout this experience. She was feeling fine after her chemo ended, in February 2019, and I didn't hear from her again until early February 2020. She returned to therapy after learning during a recent doctor's appointment that her "cancer markers were elevated." Her anxiety shot up and she wanted support.

When I heard what had happened, I asked Laura to indicate to me where on the Inner Map she was locating herself. She immediately pointed to Agitated Fear.

"What's the story you're telling yourself from this place?"

"I'm going to die," she replied.

"Well, that's quite a story! And what are you feeling right now as we talk about it?"

"My stomach is in knots and all swirly. And I notice I'm holding my breath."

Now that Laura was more focused on her sensations than on the story in her head, she began to breathe more deeply and indicated that she was starting to feel calmer.

After a couple of minutes, I said, "What seems true to me is that we don't actually know that this latest test means you're going to die." I pointed to the Map. "Where would you like to anchor yourself for now?"

At this point, Laura was able to adopt a more matter-of-fact perspective *and* a new story: "Yes…these markers came out slightly elevated, and I don't actually know what this means. It is what it is."

Laura no longer had agitated energy racing through her body, and she was able to maintain this state by repeating over and over her new story: "It is what it is, and I don't know what it means."

When I checked in with her a couple of weeks later, she reported that she'd been sustaining this neutral stance while also continuing on with her life.

What a dramatic example of how the story we tell deeply impacts our experience of ourselves and of our moment-to-moment reality. Imagine what can happen in your own life if you shift out of states Below The Line and anchor into those Above The Line as an ongoing way of interacting with the world.

Exercise: Climb the Inner Map

Using this process with clients, I've witnessed their finding peace in the throes of high agitation; a renewed sense of possibility, in despair. I myself climb the Inner Map all throughout the day.

This exercise will help you identify the level of consciousness of your major beliefs and choose a more expanded state when (1) you feel stuck in an undesirable state, (2) you notice that you're Below The Line but you don't really know why, or (3) you hear yourself telling a story that you realize (or someone points out) is Below The Line.

You sampled this exercise in Chapters 2 and 3 as we listened in on the two folks walking us, state to state, from Shame to Peace. First, here's an overview of the process:

1. Write down the issue you want to address—relationships, career, money, politics, self-image, health, your future (even death).

2. Look at the Inner Map and write out the story you have at each level of consciousness, from Shame to Peace.

3. Decide which story you most want to live from. Write it with as much detail as you can. Consider using Self-Hypnotic Induction to induce that story's state.

Now let's walk through the process with the inner voice of someone who is depressed:

1. Write down the issue you want to address—relationships, career, money, politics, self-image, health, your future (even death):

    "My life is pointless. I don't even want to get out of bed in the morning."

2. Look at the Inner Map and write out the story you have at each level of consciousness, from Shame to Peace:

    - Shame: "I am basically a bad person. That's the truth. If people get to know me, they'll figure it out, so I stay away from people."

    - Guilt: "I do bad things. I hurt people. I'm mean. Other people do good things; I'm a waste of space." (Uh-oh! A slip back to Shame. Let's keep climbing…)

    - Despair: "This has always been true. I've tried so many things to make it change, but nothing helps. I give up."

    - Sadness: "I feel so sad about it all! My heart is breaking. I miss my mother—she would understand!"

    - Frozen Fear: "I don't want to leave my house; I can't do it!"

    - Agitated Fear: "Oh, god. I have an appointment. I can't let anyone see me like this!"

    - Anger: "Yeah, well, those people have it good. They get all the breaks!"

    - Pride: "At least I'm not snotty and full of myself like they are!"

(breathe…)

- Neutrality: "My life is what it is. Life just is."

- Acceptance: "It's Monday and this is how I am. This is how my life is."

- Appreciation: "I do appreciate that I have warm clothes and an apartment. I really appreciate my dog, Buster. He's always here with me."

- Love: "Yeah, I love my dog! He's the best. When I look into his eyes, I see I'm not alone."

- Joy: "Hey, Buster, let's go out and play! It looks nice outside."

- Peace: "I see the trees and the sun and nature. I know I'm part of all of this. I know I have a place."

3. Decide which story you most want to live from. Write it with as much detail as you can. Consider using Self-Hypnotic Induction to induce that story's state.

   "I most want to live from Appreciation. I appreciate so many things—the list is endless. I appreciate four-leggeds. I appreciate what it's like to rub Buster's ears and how silky-smooth they are. I appreciate the feeling of the cold air on my cheeks and how the sun comes out and warms me up. I appreciate my lungs and breathing and how trees provide all the oxygen I need. I appreciate life!"

Notice that, at any point, this person could have taken a route back to a lower level of consciousness (probably the fiendish Upper Limit Problem rearing its head). But the idea is to stick with the story from the level you've decided to anchor into and relish the pleasure of that state.

This process is so effective, in part, because it demonstrates how every level of consciousness has its own story (and, I'd add, its own function). As people speak the belief of what is behind their current state, it's easy to see how much choice surrounds staying in that state. When I use Climb the Inner Map, I can feel the energy vortex of each level and how pulled in I am by it. The familiarity can be hard to give up! But then, the next level calls. And on up I go.

Chapter 5

Final Orienting Points

Now that we've explored the whole Inner Map, from way Below to way Above The Line, through all 14 states and their discrete functions, you've been introduced to each essential aspect of our consciousness. As you practice the exercises in Chapter 4, perhaps you're sensing the power of being able to shift your states anytime and anywhere you want. You can see how the human experience isn't static, focused on the attainment of a single state. In fact, our very aliveness can be defined by our inborn ability to constantly shift and change, expand and contract and expand again. True fulfillment of our human being-ness means being able to inhabit any state, knowing its function is a response to what the moment calls for. Full consciousness means being able to choose our focus and, ultimately, our state, versus being stuck on the automatic pilot of our unconscious processes.

The key to emotional and spiritual freedom is understanding how we unwittingly re-create old patterns when we move Below The Line. You are in your life's driver's seat, the holder of that key, and the Inner Map is your driver's manual! Strengthening your ability to observe the results you're creating and the level of consciousness of the stories behind those results is what mastery looks like.

Let's boil down everything you've learned about traversing the Inner Map:

- Identify where you are on the Inner Map.
- Value the function of the state you find yourself at.
- Notice the story you're telling that's keeping you anchored at that level of consciousness.
- Choose the state you want to anchor yourself into.

- Process the density from your current state by breathing, moving, and using other shift moves.

- Tell your new story so that you can anchor into the new, chosen state.

Embody these practices and you can create any reality you want! Once you acclimate to states that hold higher and higher vibrations, you'll find yourself collaborating with the universe as you capture the energy of those states to manifest your intentions, big and small.

Before I send you out into the world to experiment with all of this, here are some final thoughts about the landscape of the Inner Map for you to keep in mind.

Forgive the Reactive Brain, but don't let it rule you.

Poor Reactive Brain. It's doing the best it can, just trying to help you survive. It was conditioned from your birth to scan for threat, then to be ready to handle whatever comes, instantly. The fact that you're reading this means it has done its job: you've survived!

And yet, Reactive Brain is also the cause of your suffering. It has downloaded countless experiences that tell it when to react. Unfortunately, you've outgrown many of these. Do you still need to know what to do if a classmate taunts you on the playground? Is it still helping you to worry, in a meeting at work, that a tone reminiscent of your father's might lead to a beating? But there's your reactivity, telling you to be on the lookout.

If you look around, you can sense everyone else's Reactive Brain doing the same thing yours is. Bullying politicians, reckless drivers, addicts of all types—we adults are imprisoned by the patterns our Reactive Brain locked into our body very early on.

While most of us can put on a good show, appearing generally put together in public and perhaps somewhat okay in private, the deep tracks laid by Reactive Brain are inescapable in intimate relationships. Get us tired, hungry, or just plain stressed out, add in the ongoing challenges of intimacy, and Reactive Brain will come to the forefront, detecting threats that we may overestimate or even make up. Through the lens of our healing, this is actually good news: whatever is getting activated by our intimate relationships can now be acknowledged and, ideally, felt all the way through, something that wasn't possible when the threat was originally experienced in the long-ago past.

My plea is to forgive yourself, the people around you, and even me for having a Reactive Brain. We're all doing the best we can with the physiology we have. When we're activated into states Below The Line, we are not our best selves and, in fact, are capable of saying and doing things that would be unthinkable when we're Above The Line.

Still, understand what a tyrant your Reactive Brain can be when it takes over. Have a strategy for when you end up Below The Line. The dynamics of our relationships would be so much clearer if our bodies reverted to the age a trigger transports us back to: we would remember to treat ourselves (and anyone Below The Line) like a three-year-old, who, when reactive, usually just needs to eat something, drink water, take a nap, or be alone for a while. "Physiology first," I say over and over to my clients. If you're reactive, retrace your self-care tracks to see what you may have missed and can do until your body rights itself.

Being Below The Line means that the dense energies of sadness, anger, and fear are running the show. These emotions want expression! Have a good cry. Throw an old-fashioned tantrum, kicking and punching inanimate objects to your heart's content. Run around waving your hands and yelling, "FREAKOUT!" (my personal favorite way to express fear). At the very least, sit and breathe and watch the waves of dense emotional energy rise to a peak and then dissipate out of your body.[1] When we proactively take care of the basics of our physical and emotional health—paying attention to and satisfying our body's needs, noticing and constructively expressing our feelings—we optimize our chances of staying in Creative Brain. But when we inevitably tumble down to Reactive Brain, remember that there are all kinds of ways to climb back up Above The Line.

---

1 For more on how to move emotions, see my book *The Relationship Skills Workbook: A Do-It-Yourself Guide to a Thriving Relationship* (Boulder, CO: Sounds True, 2014).

Just get to the shore.

A few years back, a good friend of mine was hiking on a trail along the Poudre River outside Fort Collins. It was April, the beginning of the spring runoff, which, in Colorado, means that the river was deep, wild, and freezing-cold due to snowmelt racing down from the mountains. My friend slipped in and was instantly pulled into the raging waters on down the river.

Thankfully, she lived to tell the tale. She was in there for two to three minutes, a long time to be immersed in near-freezing water. The only thing in her mind, she told me, was "Get to the shore. Get to the shore!"

Musing on this story later, I realized what she *didn't* say to herself: "Who put this trail here!" or "I'm so stupid to have fallen in!" or "I'm gonna sue!" There was no time to blame herself or anyone else, or to make up a story. Just "Get to the shore!" And she did.

This is good wisdom if you somehow happen to fall into the rushing waters of Reactive Brain. The only thing to do is GET TO THE SHORE. Do everything, anything, to shift your physiology so that you get back Above The Line. Getting to the shore may not be easy, but it *is* simple; shift moves are limited only by your creativity. Breathe, jump, dance, play, rest, laugh, run, listen to music, chant, meditate, walk in nature, get curious about something, and on and on.[2]

Look what's not on the list above: TALKING ABOUT IT. Neither is SOLVING THE PROBLEM.

You can never solve problems with the same mindset that created them.[3] Talking, thinking, problem-solving—such brainpower is contaminated when exerted Below The Line. All there is to do is—you've got it—get to the shore. The problem will still be there, waiting patiently for you in Creative Brain, where you'll actually be capable of solving it.

---

2 For much more on shift moves, see my books *The Relationship Ride: A Usable, Unusual, Transformative Guide* (Boulder, CO: Integrity Arts Press, 2012) and *The Relationship Skills Workbook: A Do-It-Yourself Guide to a Thriving Relationship* (Boulder, CO: Sounds True, 2014).
3 Albert Einstein is likely to have said or written this, in German: *Probleme kann man niemals mit deserlben Denkweise lösen, durch die sie entstanden sind.*

Express density.

I'm not suggesting that you simply move Above The Line, tell yourself a new story, and hope for the best. To do so is to leave your body behind. "Spiritual bypassing" is what you're doing when you try to exist in a more expanded state than what your body feels, which might still be the density of states Below The Line. If you were sad, you may still have heaviness in your chest. Fear might be caught as contracted energy in your stomach or limbs. Your jaw may still be tight with anger. Shame (the combination of anger, fear, and sadness) might have spread through your whole body. Guilt, Despair, and Pride will all leave their energy trails behind.

But you don't have to stay caught in the old stories generated from those states. Once you disconnect from the story, you locate the residual energy in your body and find a constructive way to *ex-press* it, to literally push it out of your body. This is where shift moves are essential. Awareness/breath practices, energy releases, and actual physical expression through nonverbal sounding and body movement can send emotional energy through and out of your body.

View digesting emotion like digesting food.[4] Sometimes you don't even notice your digestive processes; other times, you experience digestive upset. Either way, the goal is simply to move what's being digested through and out of your body. Blaming yourself or anyone else, analyzing the contents, or talking about it at length won't hurry digestion along for either food or emotion.

Thoughts anchor; feelings flow.

We humans are extraordinarily effective at anchoring into our stories. From the myths we pass down through the ages, to the books we write, to the movies and plays we watch, to the songs we sing, to the media we surround ourselves with, we excel at storytelling and love to hear a good yarn.

---

4 According to Ayurveda, the holistic healing system from India, *ama* is the sticky substance you find on your tongue in the morning, consisting of undigested food and undigested emotion, and when it accumulates elsewhere in the body, it causes disease.

By this point, you understand the power of your thoughts (and the stories they form) to anchor you into your states, and you know that the "energy in motion" of "e-motion" can move these states through your body. You also know that you can make a conscious choice to anchor into the states you want to experience, while shifting out of the states that cause you suffering.

Remember, you are not designed to always be Above The Line. Because you are a living being in constant motion, there is no way to remain in a single state, feeling "good" all the time. You will contract into natural mammalian reactivity throughout your day, and across your lifetime. What you *can* do is consciously spend as much of your time as possible in Creative Brain by minimizing your attention on the thoughts and stories that send you into Reactive Brain. Further, be sure to do the following:

- *Use your storytelling skills wisely.*

  We all have beliefs running in the background of our consciousness. Once we track down these underground stories, we can observe how good we are at inducing, that is, hypnotizing ourselves into, whatever our current level of consciousness might be. Now that you see how good you are at storytelling, tell yourself stories that empower you.

- *Watch your language.*

  Human language is our blessing and our curse. It provides us with two tools—memory and vision—that make our human existence efficient, fruitful, and rich: we can remember our past, learning from and comforting ourselves with it; and we can imagine, plan, and analyze possibilities for our future. There is a dark side to these vast abilities, however: we may languish in past losses and perseverate about possible futures. I marvel at my dogs, thinking about their freedom from language. They never have to prove how right they are, or defend their perspective, or stay stuck in a story. Language is incredibly powerful, so do use it wisely.

Your state matters to all of us.

In *Power vs. Force*[5], Hawkins lays out the ramifications of inhabiting the states Below The Line. He believes that 85 percent of the world lives Below The Line[6], but points out that this number is counterbalanced by the vastness of the energy of the 15 percent living Above The Line. He goes on to demarcate the impact of each ascending level of consciousness. I have translated his numerical structure to the Inner Map's specific levels:

- One individual at the level of Peace counterbalances 70 million individuals Below The Line.

- One individual at the level of Joy counterbalances 10 million individuals Below The Line.

- One individual at the level of Love counterbalances 750,000 individuals Below The Line.

- One individual at the level of Appreciation counterbalances 400,000 individuals Below The Line.

- One individual at the level of Acceptance counterbalances 90,000 individuals Below The Line.

In these days of rapid social, economic, environmental, and political change, any rectifying action can seem minuscule and inconsequential in the face of such overwhelming global challenges. Hawkins' figures, however, show that each and every one of us has great power in our hands—well, in our whole body! It's a matter of choosing what level you want to commit to and taking the actions—shifting your body, telling expansive, Above-The-Line stories—that will anchor you there. Or, as I say over and over, "Be an activist! Choose Love."

Your stories create your world.

Now that you are more conscious of your abilities as a storyteller, you

---

5 David R. Hawkins, M.D., Ph.D., *Power vs. Force: The Hidden Determinants of Human Behavior: An Anatomy of Consciousness* (Carlsbad, CA: Hay House, Inc., 2002), p. 282.
6 When I saw Hawkins speak in 2014, he had revised that number to 75 percent, citing the impact of the 2012 Harmonic Convergence on humanity's consciousness.

can use your gift of language to generate narratives of the world you want to live in, internally and externally. Your language generates your state, which generates your language, which generates your state, on and on and on. Hop onto this merry-go-round of consciousness, recognizing that you—one storyteller in a global collective of storytellers—can make a difference if you remember these caveats:

- *Nothing is true; everything is true. It's all how you tell the story.*

    When I was a child, I read voraciously. I loved existing in different times and places. I didn't realize, until I was an adult, that none of the stories were "true." I was shocked. I'd thought there was a "there" out there. Now I understand that perhaps every story is "true"—a version of reality that the storyteller has landed on, that draws the rest of us in.

    Every socially sanctioned atrocity and every brutal power system relies on some people's ability to weave a narrative that draws others in. War, genocide, oppression of entire peoples, racism, sexism, classism—all of these global ills are justified by the stories humans tell and enroll others in. The good news is that every political and social movement rests on this human capability as well; our evolution as a species has depended on the visionary storytelling of masters throughout the ages. Stories that enslave can give way to stories that liberate all beings.

- *No one in Reactive Brain believes in equality.*

    Across the globe, even the most democratic nations still wobble between political ideals and the persistent realities of income inequality, racism, sexism, and classism. None of these societal tensions will be solved in Reactive Brain because, at its essence, Reactive Brain is hierarchy. Instantly—in Pride and Anger—we dominate. Immediately—in Agitated Fear, Frozen Fear, Sadness, Despair, Guilt, and Shame—we flee or freeze or faint. Naturally, in those states, from our position of Power Up or Power Down, we will see the world only through hierarchy. We humans will not reach a consensus, that is, a new collective story about equality, until we are able to disbelieve the stories generated by Reactive

Brain and weave our shared experiences of Creative Brain into a sustainable collective reality.

- *You must commit to living Above The Line.*

Currently, per Hawkins' figure, many members of our species live Below The Line much of the time. As one who now understands the Inner Map and its effects, consider committing to living Above The Line. Such a commitment isn't a promise that you'll always be Above The Line—you're human, after all. To commit is to "organize your energies towards"; you can recommit as many times as it takes.[7]

Our results signal what we're committed to. Given what humankind has created in this world, it is clear that we have long been committed to living Below The Line. Your living Above The Line, from Creative Brain, is a radical act that generates a seismic shift in consciousness. Embodying this evolutionary power is what will transform our species and the planet.

Together, our stories create the world's story.

I deeply appreciate you for being a fellow journeyer on this road to human evolution. I understand how challenging these practices can be; I also experience ongoingly how richly rewarding they are. *The Inner Map: Navigating Your Emotions to Create the World You Want* is meant to be a handbook, full of road signs and reminders as you honor your commitment to live Above The Line. Know that you are not alone; many of us are stepping into the new realms revealed from the incredibly high vibrations of the consciousness of Creative Brain. In fact, I coined the term "evolutionary power" for living from these levels, as I view this realm as the next stage in human evolution. Appendix II presents the Four Cornerstones of Evolutionary Power, with guidelines per cornerstone for sustaining a life Above The Line.

We are living in extraordinary times. Faced with unprecedented challenges, we can easily become discouraged, believing that what's in front of us is unsolvable, that humans don't have the resources to handle what's ahead.

---

7 Gay Hendricks, Ph.D., *Conscious Living: Finding Joy in the Real World* (New York: HarperCollins, 2000).

But that's just a story, anchored somewhere Below The Line. Is it true? Well, of course it's true. But it isn't any truer than this story I want to tell you:

> Humans are naturally good, loving beings. Every breath we take is filled with joy; the very air we breathe is infused with love. As we walk across this planet together, we link arms to solve every problem facing us, with innovative solutions generated through our amazing ability to collaborate with one another. We connect deeply with ourselves, with all other beings, and with the energies of nature, seen and unseen. Our cells interlock at the highest levels, allowing previously unimaginable communication and possibilities to emerge. We co-create with the universe. We finally know ourselves—and all that is—as truly divine.

I am living into *that* story.

Appendix I

Functions of Levels of Consciousness

Qualities of Being in Reactive Brain (aka, Below The Line)

- You have a narrow focus; your attention is on what is "wrong."
- You have a sense of immediacy and urgency.
- Your thinking is stereotypical and concrete.
- You're basically "cognitively disabled," as your body puts its resources into fighting, fleeing, or freezing from the threat.
- Your energy, while initially charged up to respond to threat, is ultimately being depleted.
- Your body is in a stress response, releasing a surge of hormones, predominately adrenaline, cortisol, and norepinephrine.
- Your immediate focus is on what the threat is and who is causing that threat (i.e., who is to blame).
- Your speaking rhythm changes: either it speeds up and sounds forceful or language is hard to find and hard to generate.
- Life seems difficult, full of effort and struggle, as you are existing in a field of resistance.
- You feel disconnected from others.
- You perceive the world through a lens of competition, scarcity, and unfriendliness.

Qualities of Being in Creative Brain (aka, Above The Line)

- Your focus will be open while your attention tunes in to what is "right."

- You experience time as slowing down and expanding.

- The quality of your thinking is optimized, allowing you to generate new possibilities and innovative ideas.

- Your energy is being continuously regenerated.

- Your body is in a relaxed, rebuilding response, as cells can shift away from protection and into regeneration.

- Your speaking pace is natural, easy, and unpressured.

- You perceive others as safe, as potential collaborators and allies.

- You're in a field of expansiveness, in ease and flow; life unfolds with serendipity.

- Your sense of connection with others is enhanced.

- You perceive the world as being full of kinship, abundance, and friendliness.

Specific Reactive Brain Functions

State	Function
Pride (mobilized anger)	• Main function: Solidify alpha status • Maintains alpha status without resorting to pure aggression • Polar opposite of Shame, so much motivation to stay out of Shame (fighting not to be right but to be not wrong)
Anger	• Main function: Directly establish and maintain the status of the alpha through pure, direct, mobilized aggression • Energy of domination
Agitated Fear	• Main function: Get to safety • Tremendously functional response to being threatened: flee

Frozen Fear	• Main functions:
	  ▪ Stop forward movement
	  ▪ Orient to threat
	  ▪ Find and obey alpha
	• First step into immobilization

Sadness	• Main function: Protest loss of valued connection and create reconnection • Immobilization communicates submission but allows for crying out
Despair (immobilized sadness)	• Main function: Abandon protest about lost connection and prepare for death • Looks like depression

Guilt (immobilized fear + anger)	• Main functions:
	  ▪ Immobilize own impulses so as to regain alpha's good graces (and thus access to resources)
	  ▪ Avoid loss and negative "correction" from alpha
	• Aggression now going inward

Shame (immobilized fear + anger + sadness)	• Main function: Energetically freeze (collapse) self to ward off aggression and/or loss of alpha • Direct result of aggression and contempt from Power Up • Aggression now directed at self to halt actual trajectory of aggression towards alpha

Specific Creative Brain Functions

State	Function
Neutrality	Face into what is
Acceptance	Accept what is
Appreciation	Orient to the positive of what is
Love	Join with the energy of the universe to co-create
Joy	Celebrate life
Peace	Exist as one with all

Appendix II

Four Cornerstones of Evolutionary Power

What is "evolutionary power"? I define it as this: living in flow and from essence, thereby manifesting outcomes consciously and directly, ultimately resulting in a life that is a walking expression of one's deepest self.

Evolutionary power supersedes the traditional paradigm that defines power as domination and control, which necessarily relies on the submission of others. Evolutionary power is the collective energy that supports humanity in transcending the limitations of hierarchy and living into our true potential. Evolutionary power—also known as co-creativity and "power with"—upholds the equal value of all human beings and the optimization of every person's functioning. Evolutionary power exists in a field of nonresistance; creates an environment of optimal cognitive functioning, creativity, and healthy; and supports the way we live our best lives: in connection.

The Four Cornerstones of Evolutionary Power is a guide to the perspectives and stances we can take to live into our best selves. My future work will facilitate the embodiment of every aspect of these four cornerstones, summarized in the chart on the next page and also available as a downloadable, printable PDF at www.JuliaColwell.com/Books.

LIVING IN ALIGNMENT + FLOW	**USING TOOLS TO SUPPORT EXPANSIVE LIVING**
<ul><li>I know my purpose.</li><li>My manifesto/commitments/intentions are clear and available to me at all times; my life and my self reflect these.</li><li>My essence is palpable.</li><li>I am in energetic balance.</li><li>I love myself deeply and continuously.</li><li>I relate to myself compassionately.</li><li>I know what I really want, and I live intentionally from what I really want.</li><li>I understand flow, how to co-create it, and how to surf it.</li><li>I connect with others from Creative Brain, always looking for the answer to "How can everybody get everything they want?"</li></ul>	<ul><li>I use a variety of tools that reliably move density out of my body.</li><li>I connect to energy fields of high vibration.</li><li>I seek feedback and respond to it with openness and agility.</li><li>I choose to interpret my experiences through the most expansive story I can create.</li><li>I cultivate neutrality, acceptance, appreciation, love, joy, and peace.</li><li>I have a daily practice of prayer and meditation.</li><li>I take care of myself exquisitely.</li><li>I own my projections and wonder about them: What is the feedback I'm creating for myself?</li><li>I value being challenged by relationships as a path to moving dense energy out of my body.</li></ul>
RESONATING IN A HIGH ENERGY FIELD	**CULTIVATING AN OPEN HEART**
<ul><li>I know I live in a friendly universe where life is unfolding perfectly.</li><li>What I absorb has high vibration (food, air, substances, thoughts, words, music, relationships, experiences, media).</li><li>What I generate has high vibration (thoughts, words, expression).</li><li>I know myself to be the source of my ongoing experience.</li><li>I have an ongoing connection to Source.</li><li>I notice and co-create with the magic that is all around me.</li></ul>	<ul><li>I accept, appreciate, and love what is.</li><li>I choose to keep my heart open.</li><li>I live from service.</li><li>I embrace all states of consciousness, knowing them all as divine.</li></ul>

About the Author

Julia B. Colwell, Ph.D., is a traditionally trained clinical psychologist, having learned Freud's principles and psychodynamic theory while simultaneously being influenced by feminist theory and the gay rights movement in the '70s and '80s. After graduate school, she was introduced to body-centered theory and suddenly woke up in a whole different world, one where the question turned from "How do I assess what is wrong in people?" to "How can I support people to feel as good as possible?"

Photo: Jewel Afflerbaugh

Julie is the founder of the Evolutionary Power Institute, in Boulder, Colorado, where she sees clients, teaches workshops, runs intensive groups, and spreads the word, to as many people as she can, about what the embodiment of true power looks like. She lives in Boulder with her wife of 32 years and their three adopted canines.

www.JuliaColwell.com

www.ingramcontent.com/pod-product-compliance
Lightning Source LLC
Chambersburg PA
CBHW062027290426
44108CB00025B/2813